FOR ORGANS, PIANOS & ELECTRONIC KEYBOARDS

E-Z PLAY TODAY

49

Disney

Beauty and the Beast

MUSIC FROM THE MOTION PICTURE SOUNDTRACK

Music by ALAN MENKEN
Lyrics by HOWARD ASHMAN and TIM RICE

ISBN 978-1-4950-9620-4

Wonderland Music Company, Inc.
Walt Disney Music Company

DISTRIBUTED BY

HAL•LEONARD®

7777 W. BLUEMOUND RD. P.O. BOX 13819 MILWAUKEE, WI 53213

In Australia Contact:
Hal Leonard Australia Pty. Ltd.
4 Lentara Court
Cheltenham, Victoria, 3192 Australia
Email: ausadmin@halleonard.com.au

Visit Hal Leonard Online at
www.halleonard.com

Aria

Registration 2
Rhythm: Waltz

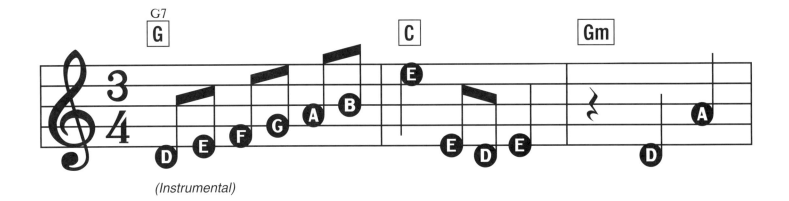

(Instrumental)

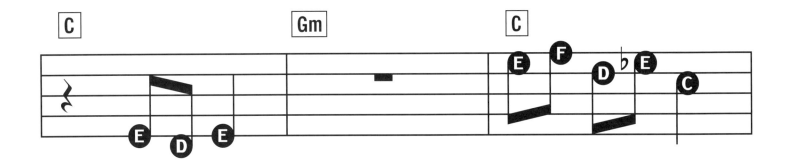

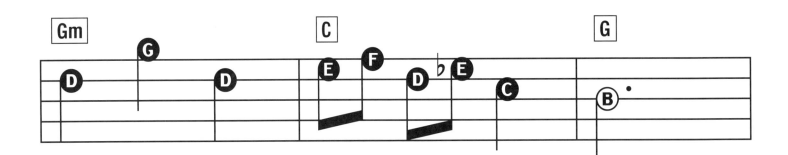

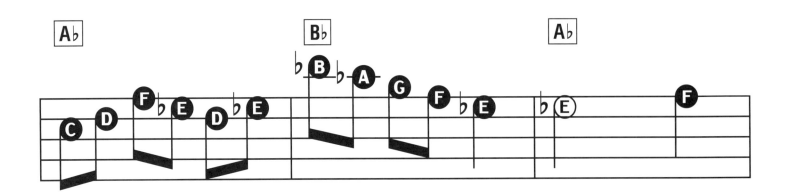

Music by Alan Menken
Lyrics by Tim Rice

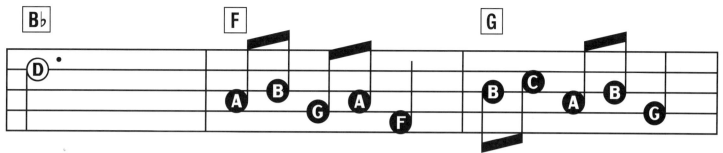

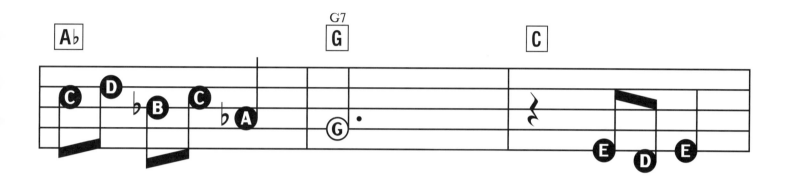

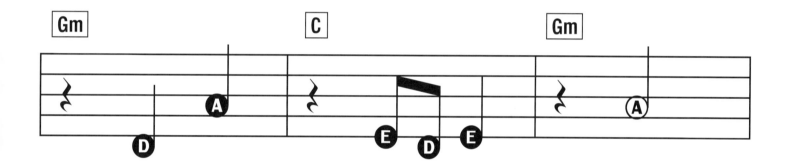

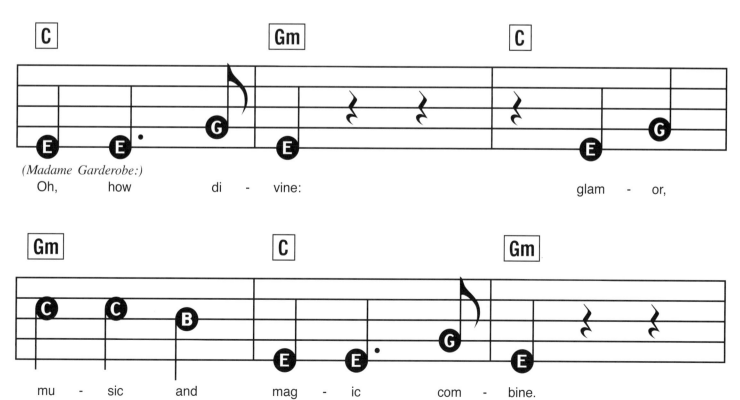

(Madame Garderobe:)
Oh, how di - vine: glam - or,

mu - sic and mag - ic com - bine.

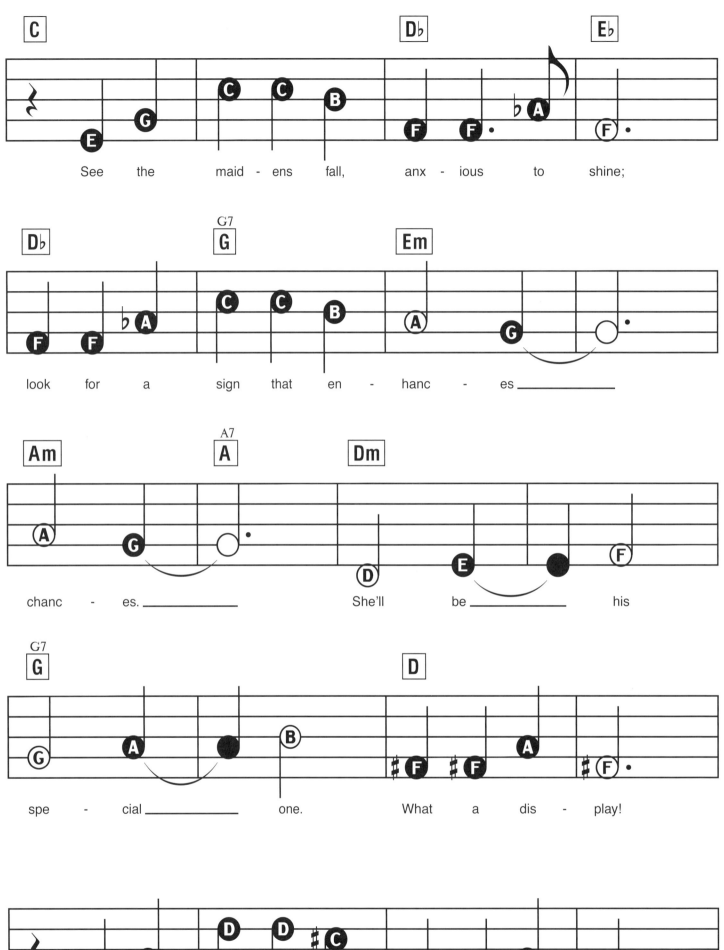

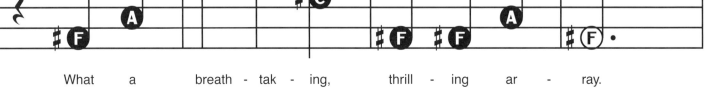

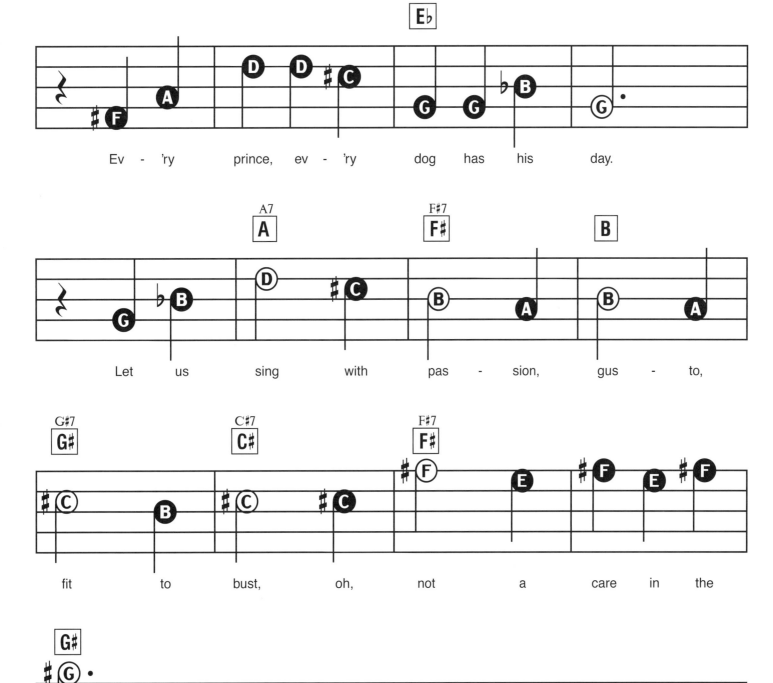

Ev - 'ry prince, ev - 'ry dog has his day.

Let us sing with pas - sion, gus - to,

fit to bust, oh, not a care in the

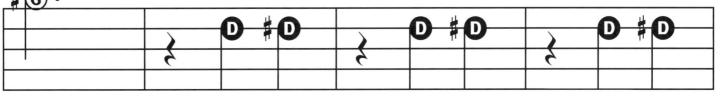

world. *(Instrumental)*

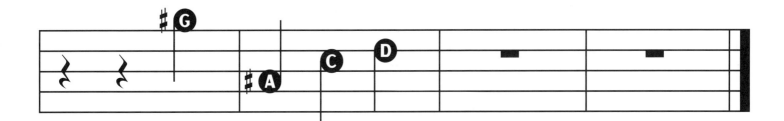

Belle

Registration 9
Rhythm: March or Polka

Music by Alan Menken
Lyrics by Howard Ashman

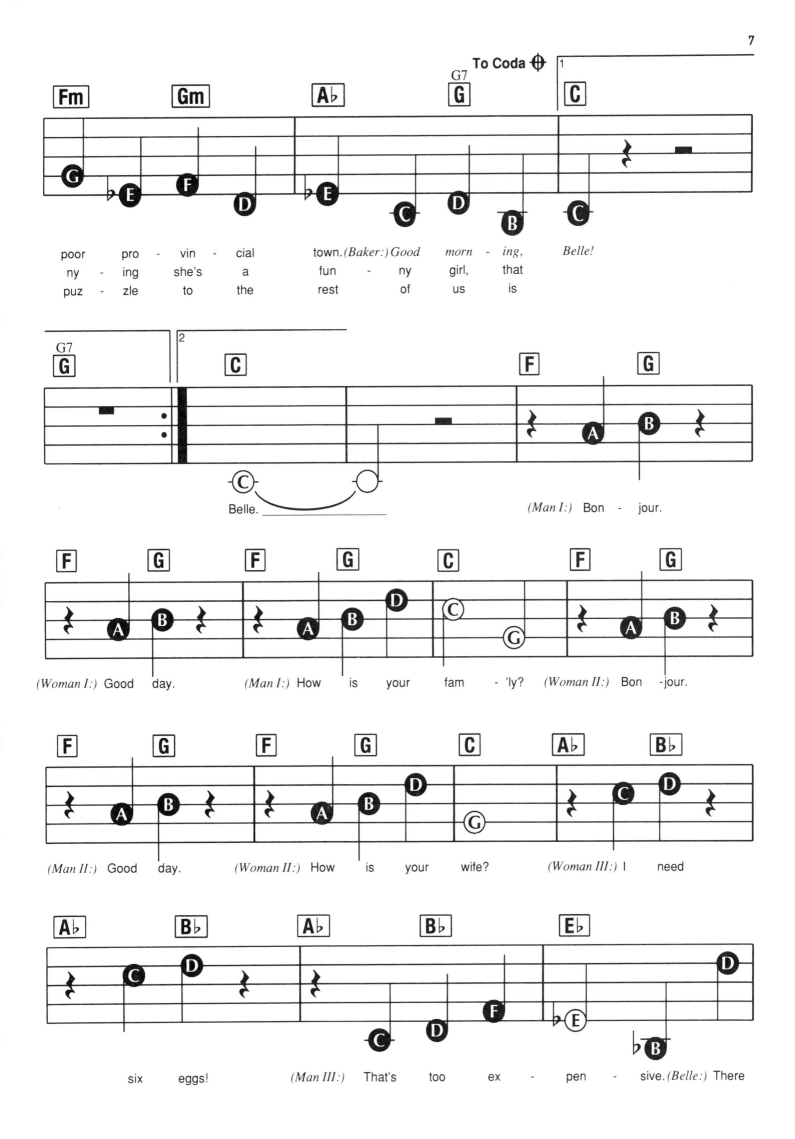

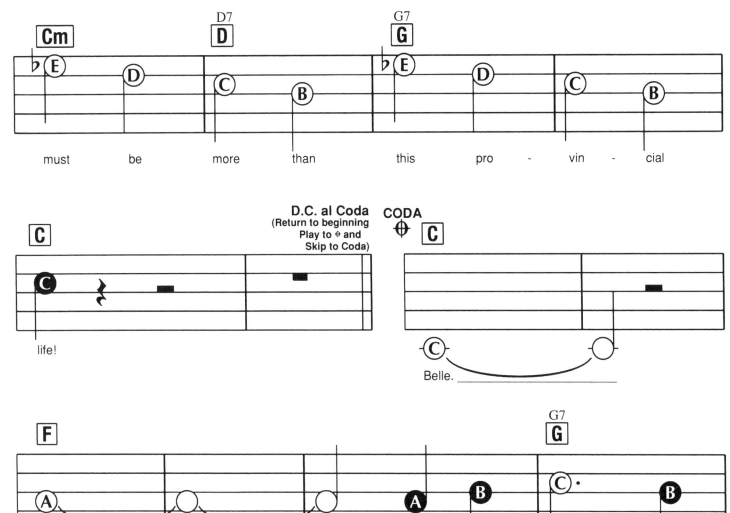

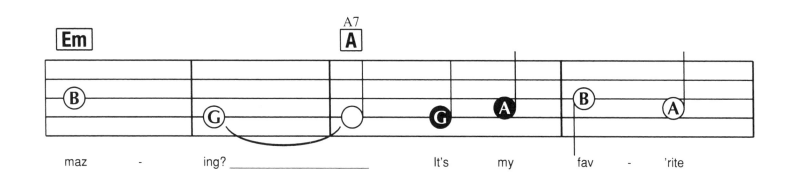

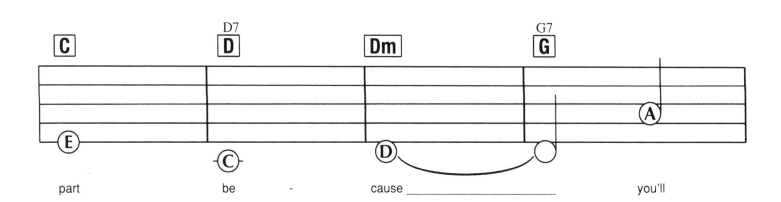

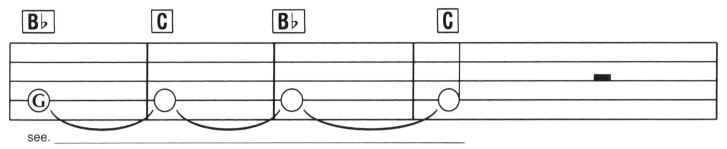

see.

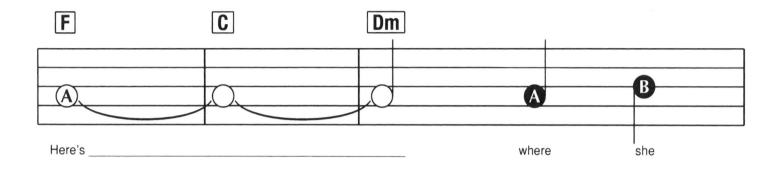

Here's   where   she

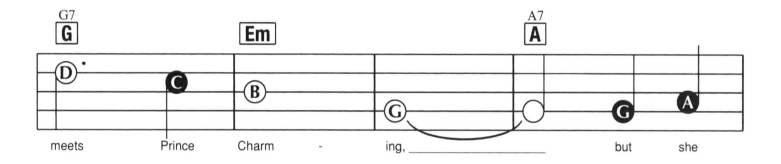

meets   Prince   Charm - ing,   but   she

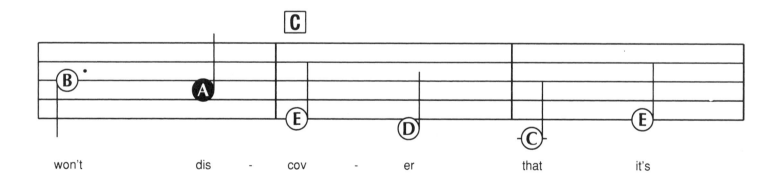

won't   dis - cov - er   that   it's

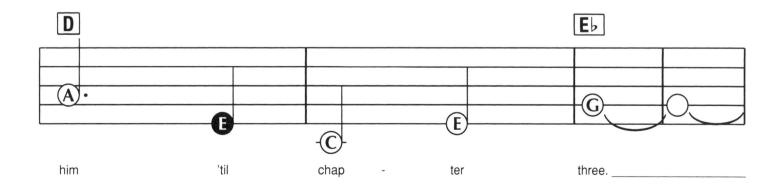

him   'til   chap - ter   three.

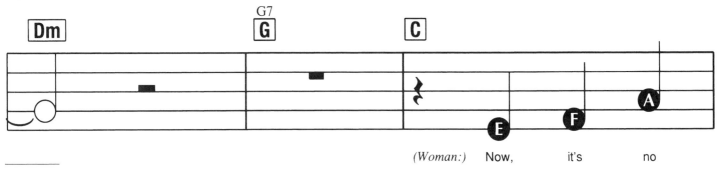

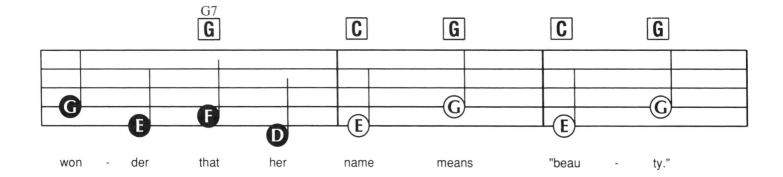

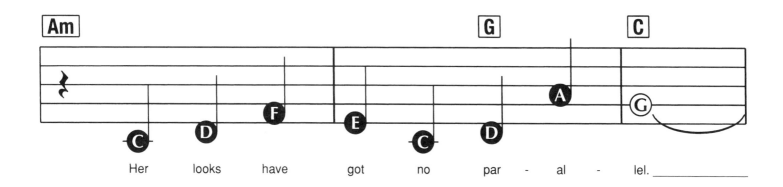

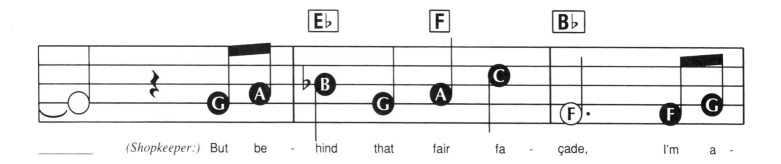

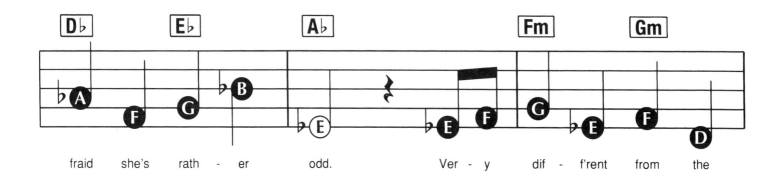

11

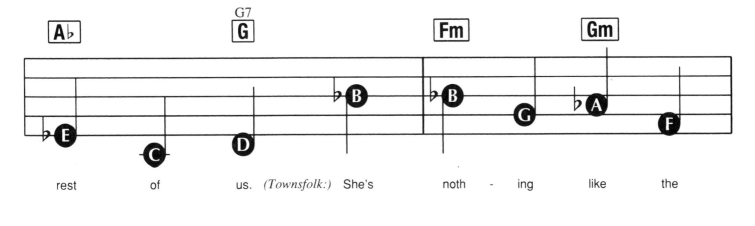

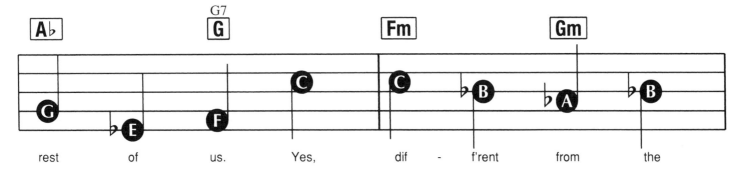

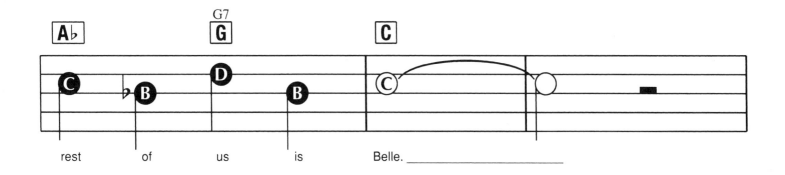

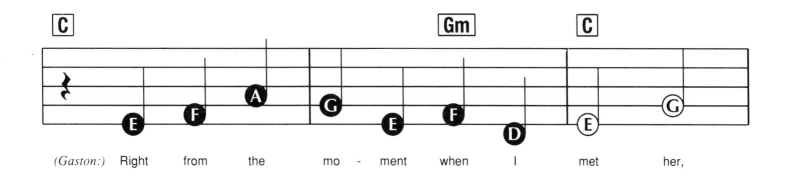

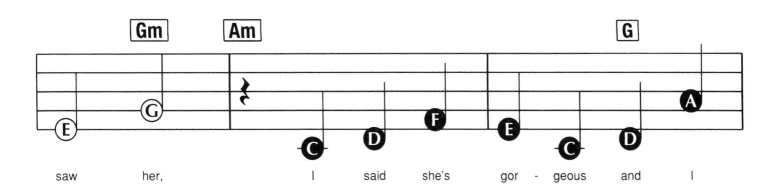

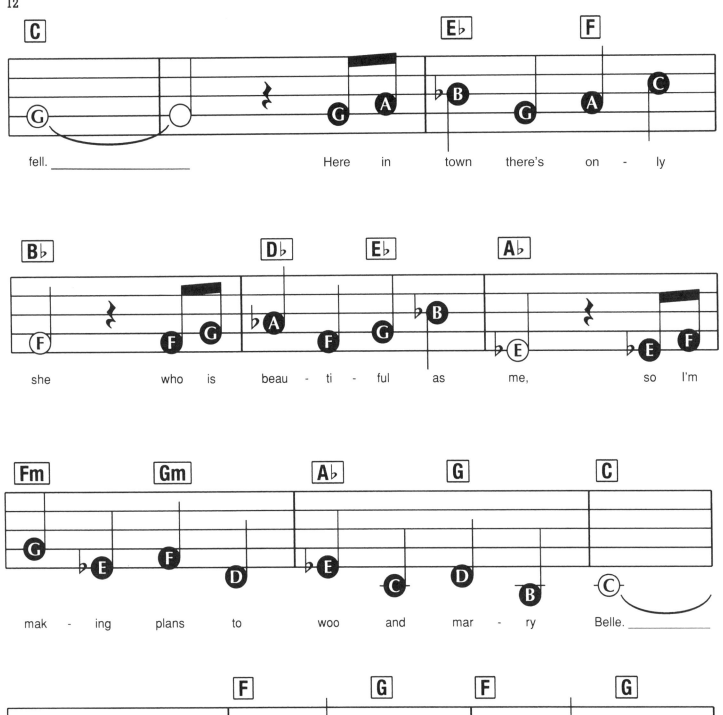

fell. _____ Here in town there's on - ly

she who is beau - ti - ful as me, so I'm

mak - ing plans to woo and mar - ry Belle. _____

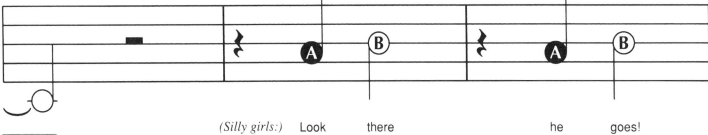

(Silly girls:) Look there he goes!

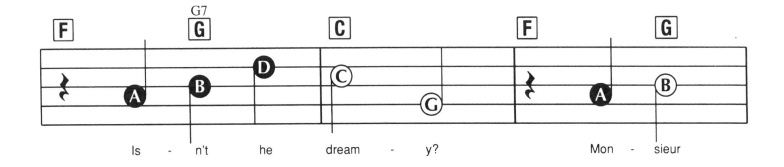

Is - n't he dream - y? Mon - sieur

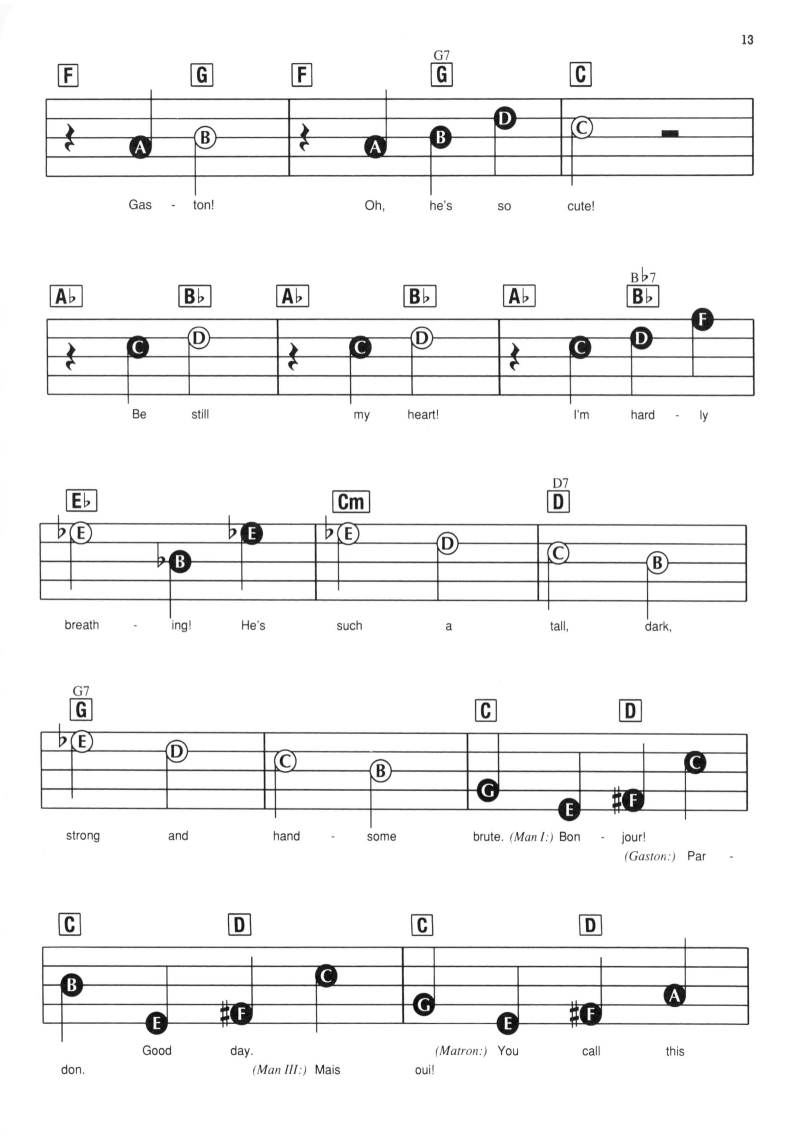

13

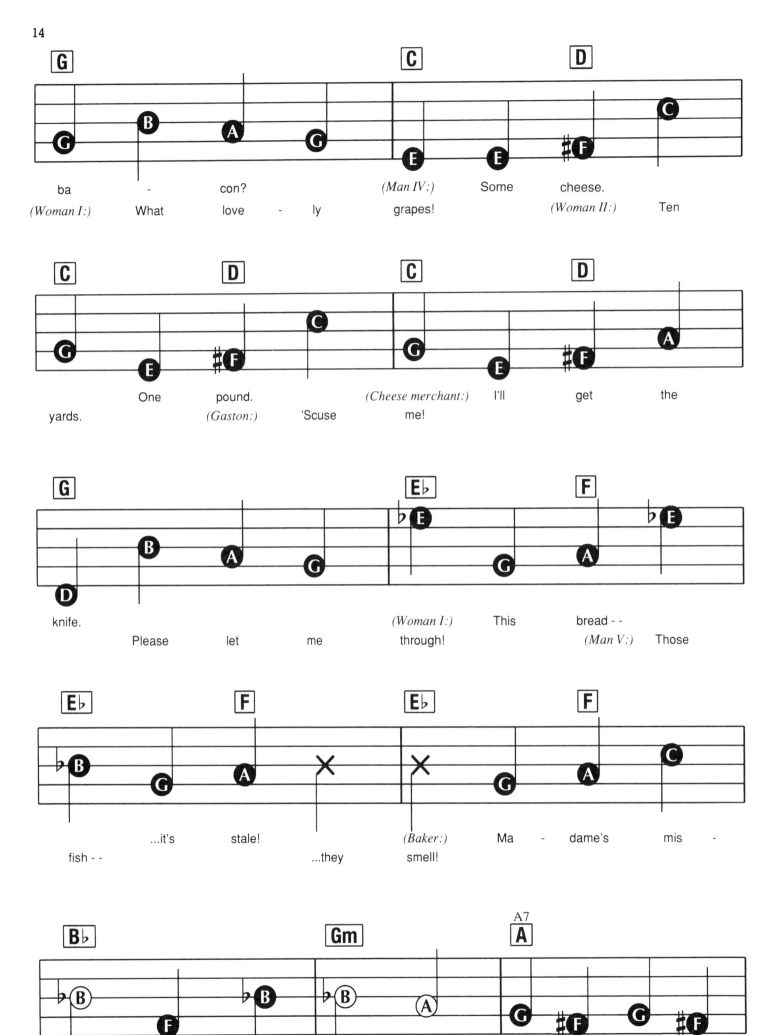

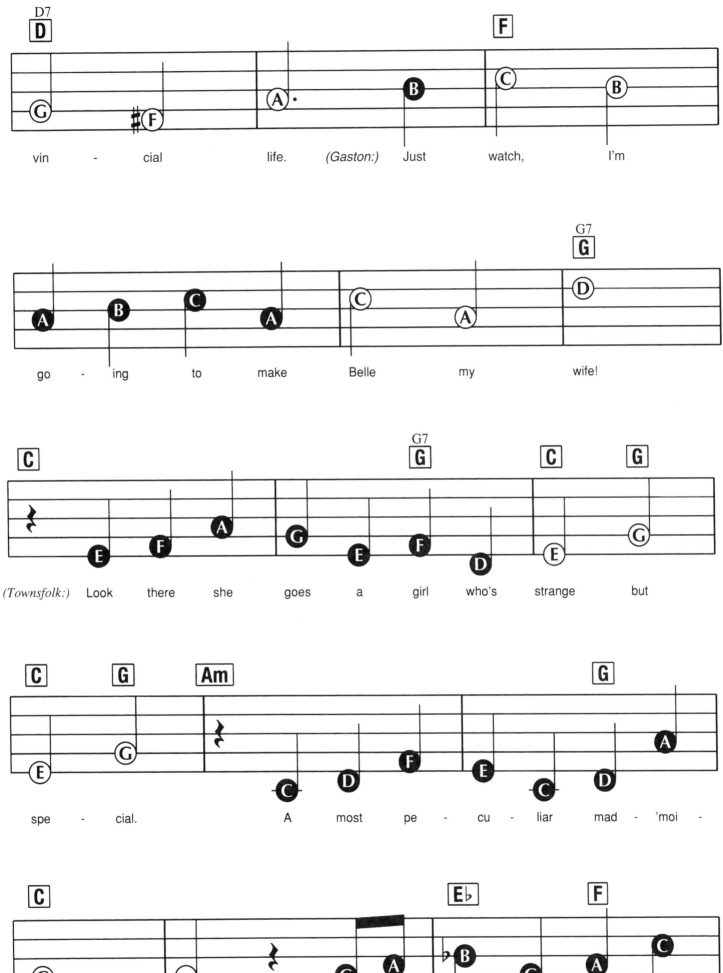

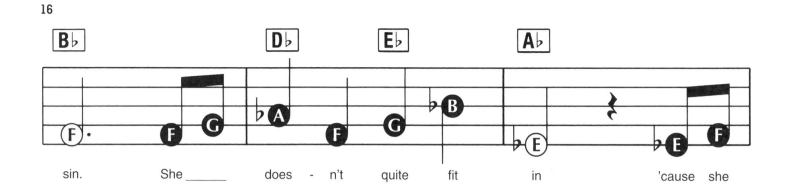

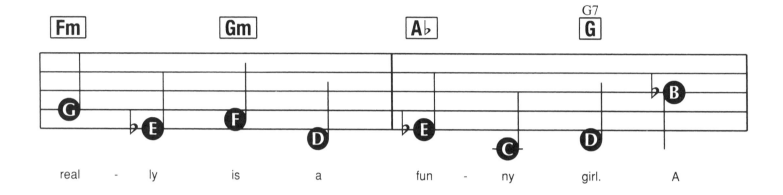

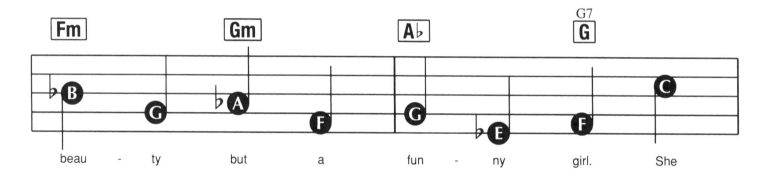

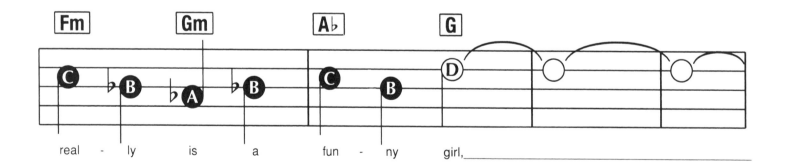

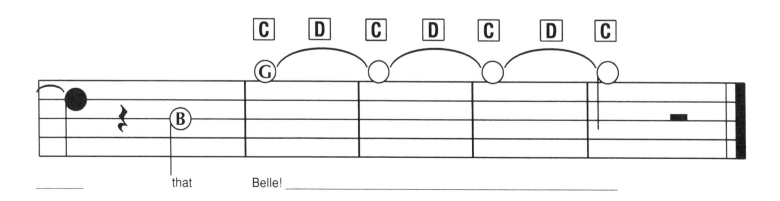

How Does a Moment Last Forever

Registration 1
Rhythm: Broadway or Ballad

Music by Alan Menken
Lyrics by Tim Rice

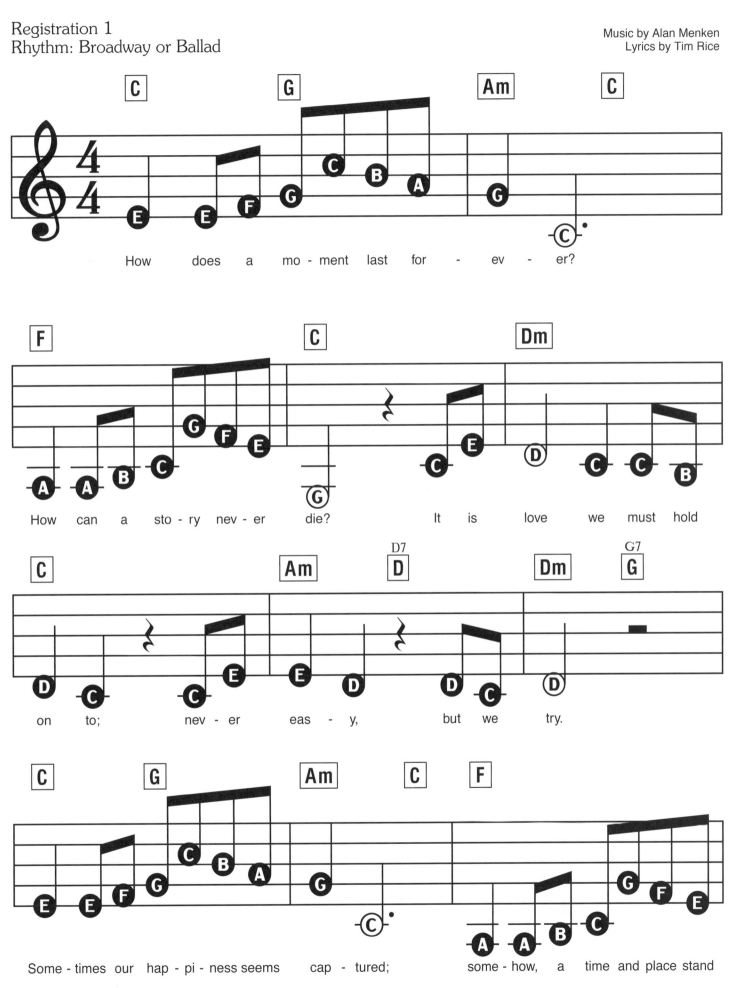

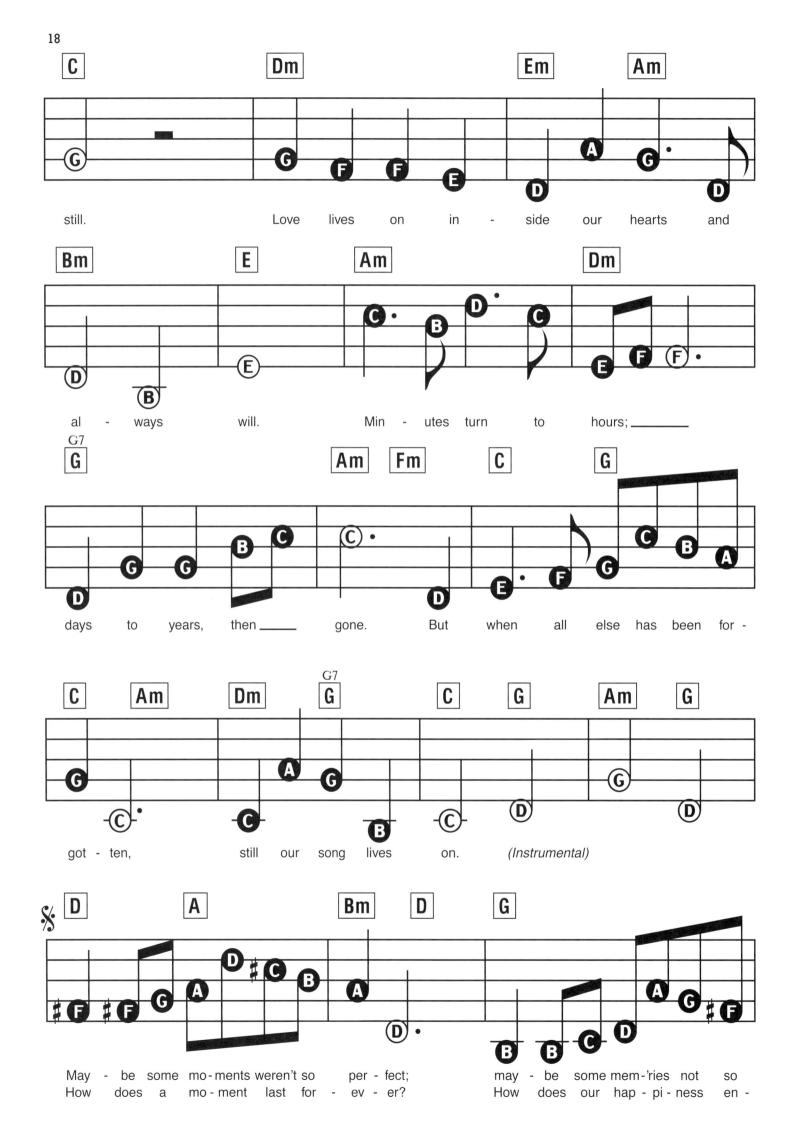

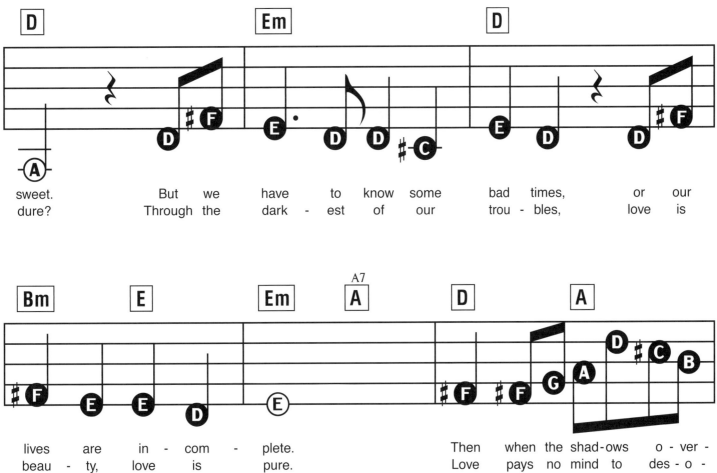

sweet.   But we have to know some bad times, or our
dure?   Through the dark - est of our trou - bles, love is

lives are in - com - plete.   Then when the shad-ows o - ver -
beau - ty, love is pure.   Love pays no mind to des - o -

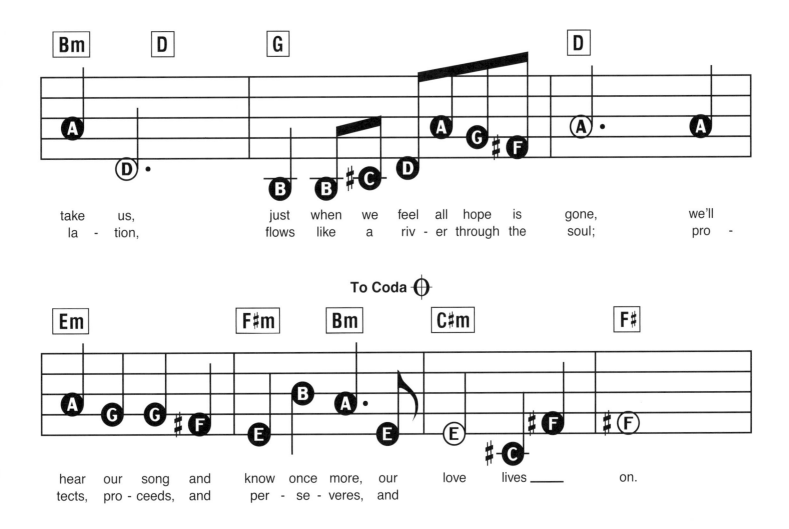

take us,   just when we feel all hope is gone, we'll
la - tion,   flows like a riv - er through the soul; pro -

To Coda ⊕

hear our song and know once more, our love lives _____ on.
tects, pro - ceeds, and per - se - veres, and

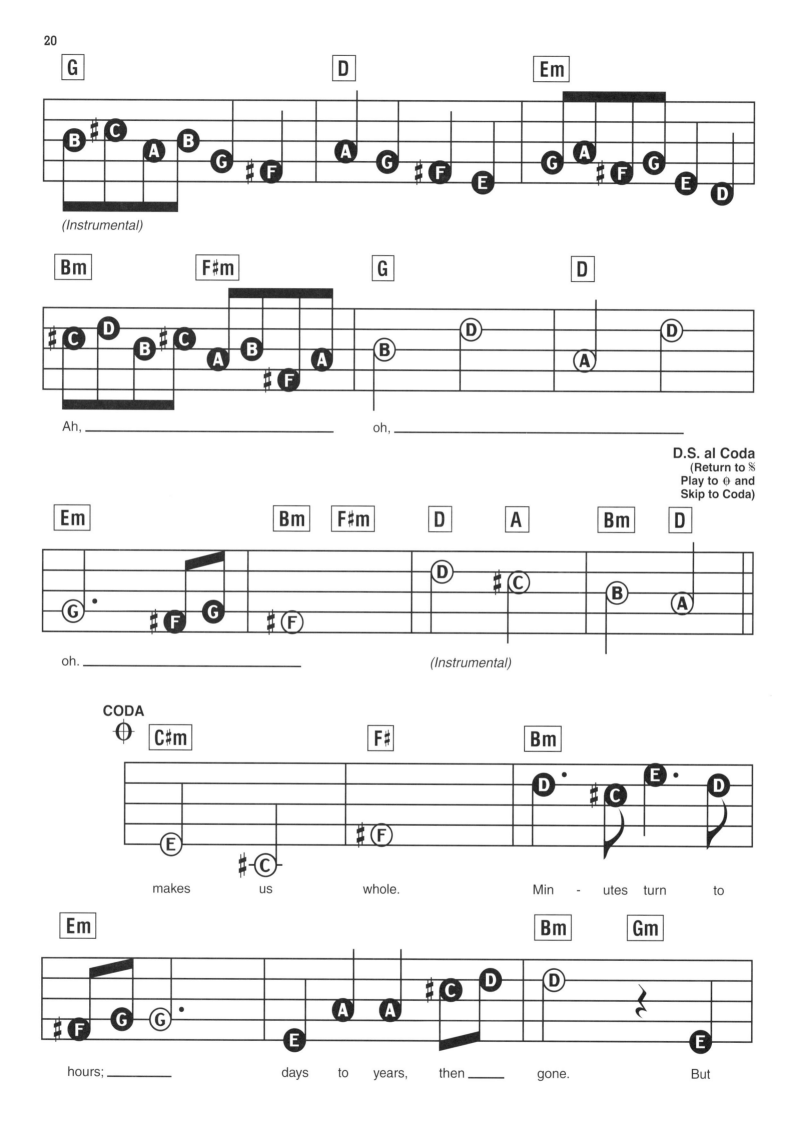

(Instrumental)

Ah, _____ oh, _____

D.S. al Coda
(Return to 𝄋
Play to ⊕ and
Skip to Coda)

oh. _____ (Instrumental)

CODA

makes   us   whole.   Min - utes turn to

hours; _____ days   to   years,   then _____ gone.   But

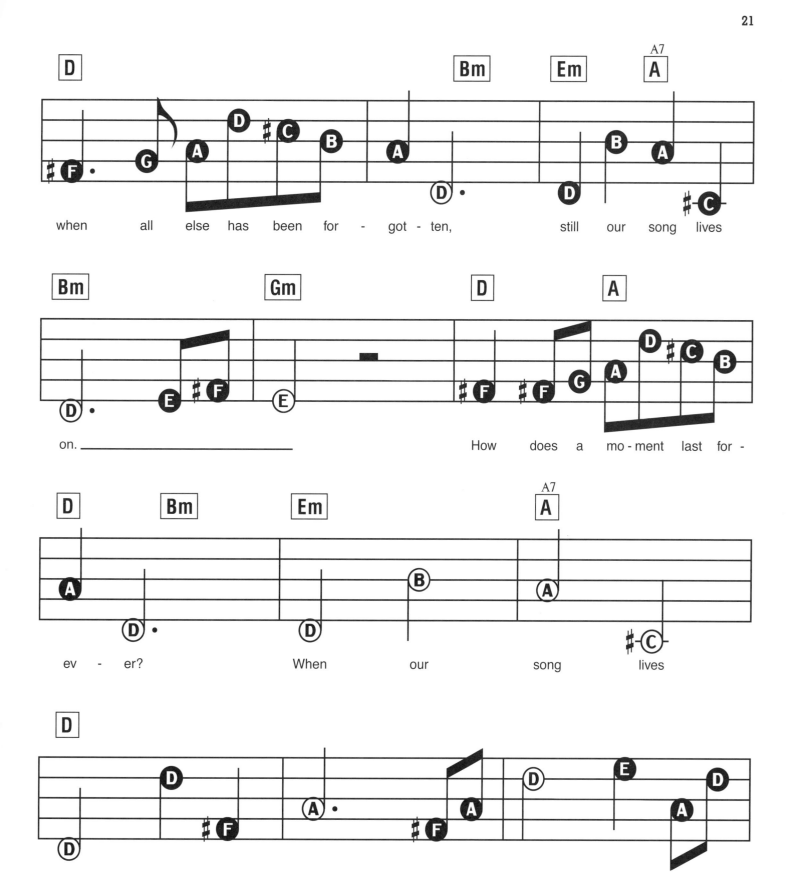

when all else has been for - got - ten, still our song lives

on. How does a mo - ment last for -

ev - er? When our song lives

on! *(Instrumental)*

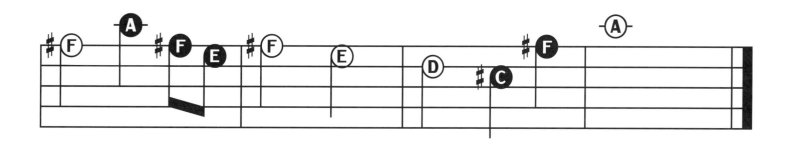

Gaston

Registration 3
Rhythm: Waltz

Music by Alan Menken
Lyrics by Howard Ashman

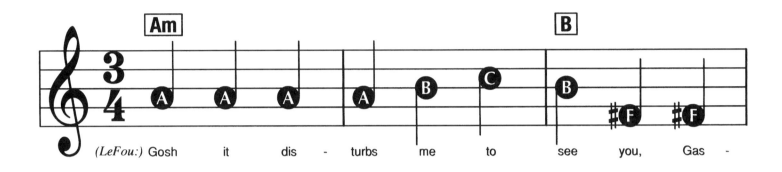

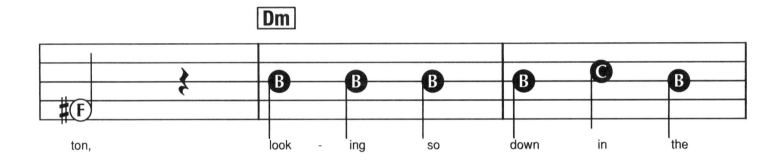

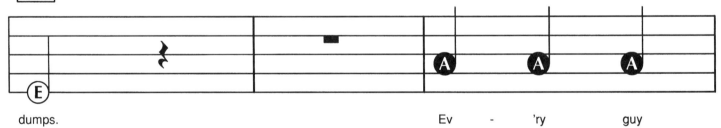

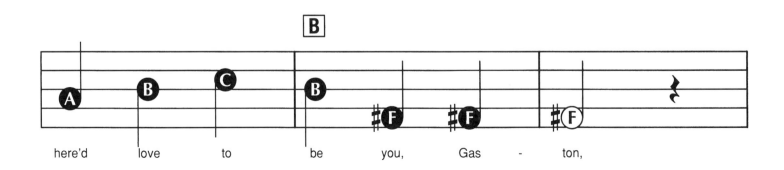

23

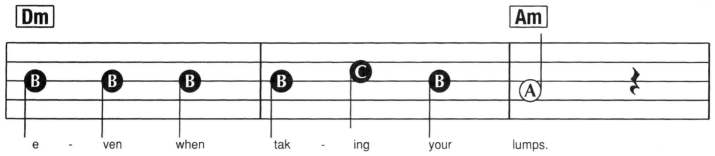

e - ven when tak - ing your lumps.

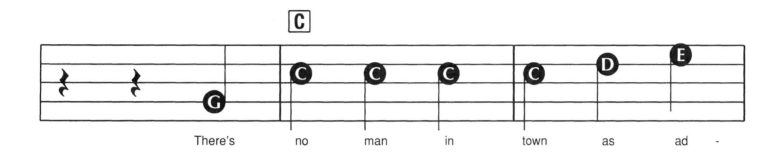

There's no man in town as ad -

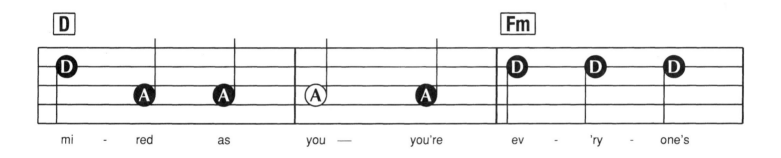

mi - red as you — you're ev - 'ry - one's

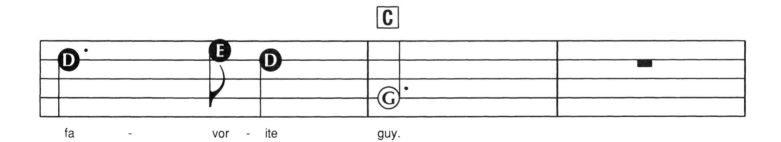

fa - vor - ite guy.

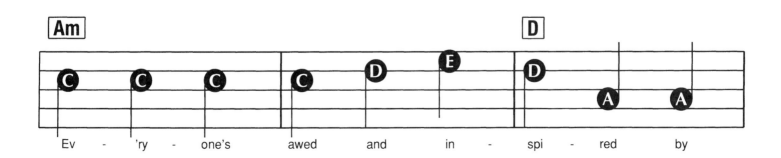

Ev - 'ry - one's awed and in - spi - red by

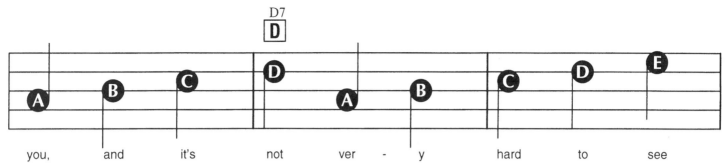

you, and it's not ver - y hard to see

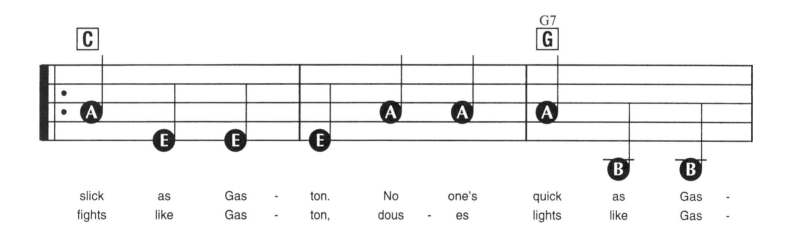

why. _____ No one's

slick as Gas - ton. No one's quick as Gas -
fights like Gas - ton, dous - es lights like Gas -

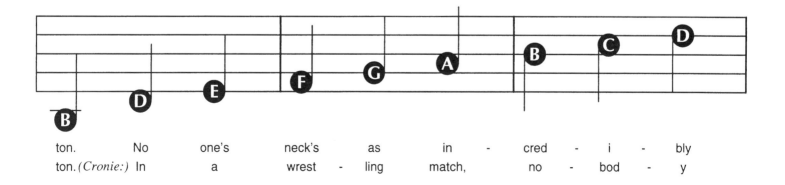

ton. No one's neck's as in - cred - i - bly
ton. *(Cronie:)* In a wrest - ling match, no - bod - y

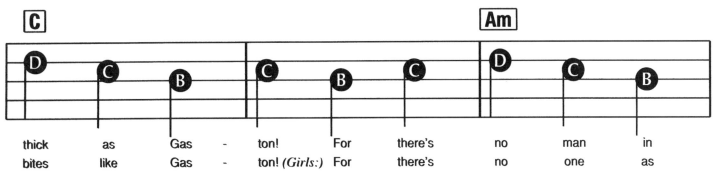

C   **Am**

| thick | as | Gas | - | ton! | For | there's | no | man | in |
| bites | like | Gas | - | ton! *(Girls:)* | For | there's | no | one | as |

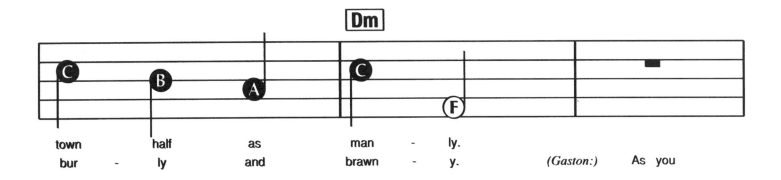

Dm

| town | half | as | man | - | ly. | |
| bur | - ly | as | and | brawn | - y. | *(Gaston:)* As you |

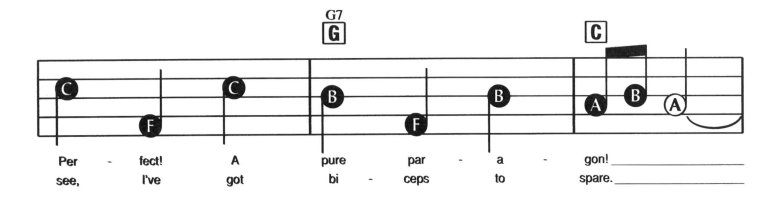

G7 / **G**   **C**

| Per | - fect! | A | pure | par | - a | - gon! _____ |
| see, | I've | got | bi | - ceps | to | spare. _____ |

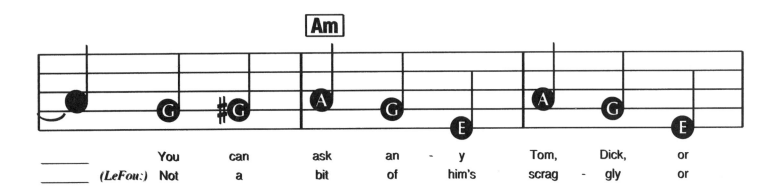

Am

| _____ | You | can | ask | an | - y | Tom, | Dick, | or |
| _____ *(LeFou:)* Not | a | bit | of | him's | scrag | - gly | or |

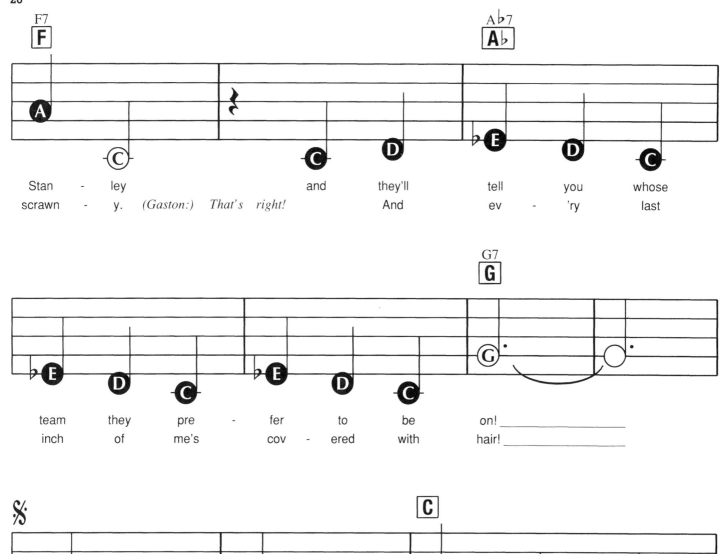

Stan - ley | and | they'll | tell | you | whose
scrawn - y. *(Gaston:) That's right!* | And | ev - 'ry | last

team | they | pre - fer | to | be | on! _____
inch | of | me's | cov - ered | with | hair! _____

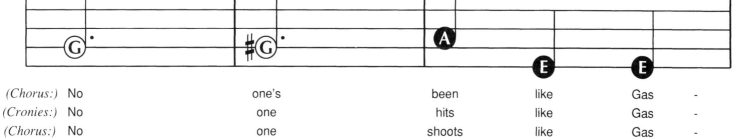

(Chorus:) No | one's | been | like | Gas -
(Cronies:) No | one | hits | like | Gas -
(Chorus:) No | one | shoots | like | Gas -

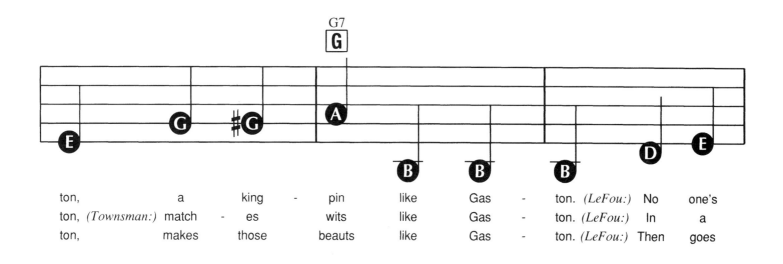

ton, | a | king - pin | like | Gas - ton. *(LeFou:)* No | one's
ton, *(Townsman:)* match - es | wits | like | Gas - ton. *(LeFou:)* In | a
ton, | makes | those | beauts | like | Gas - ton. *(LeFou:)* Then | goes

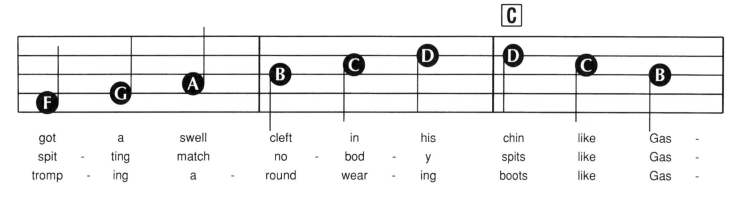
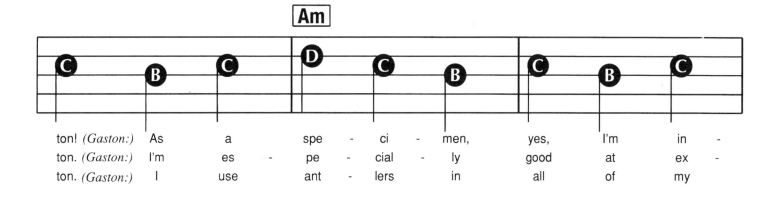
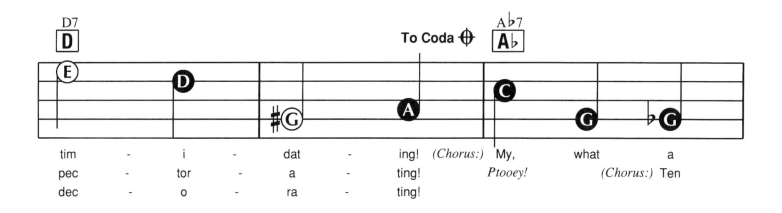
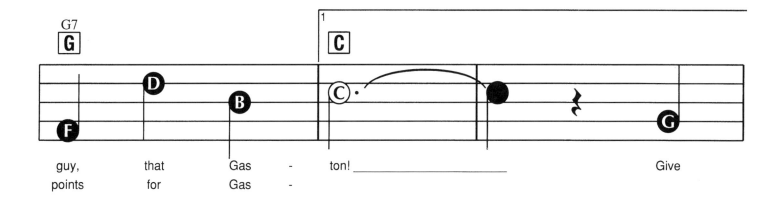

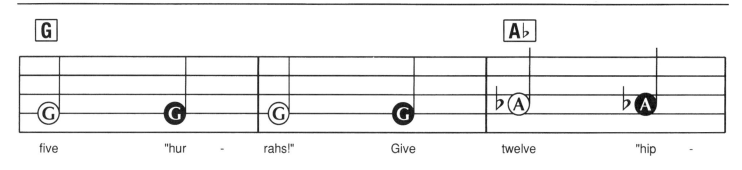

five   "hur - rahs!"   Give   twelve   "hip -

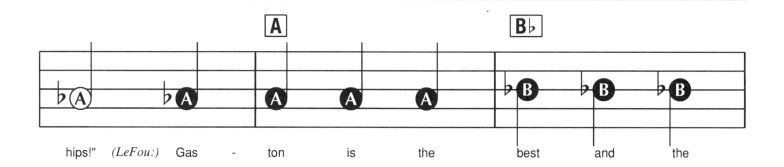

hips!"   *(LeFou:)*   Gas - ton   is   the   best   and   the

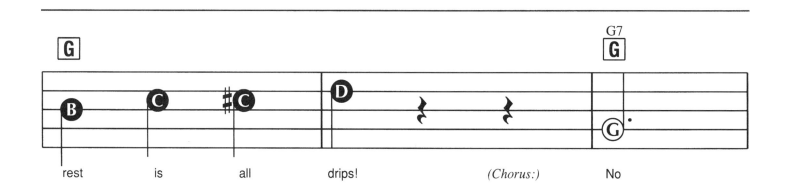

rest   is   all   drips!   *(Chorus:)*   No

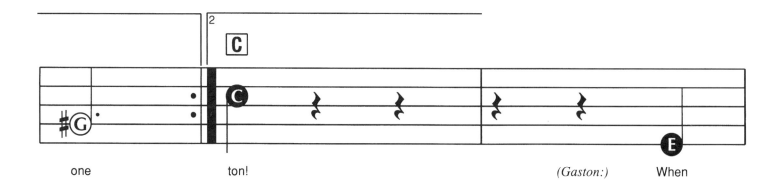

one   ton!   *(Gaston:)*   When

29

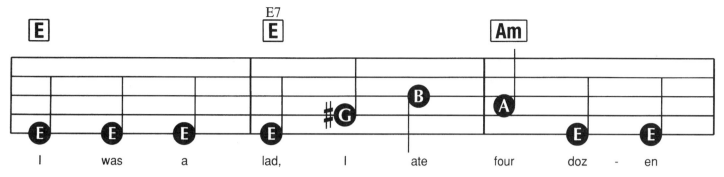

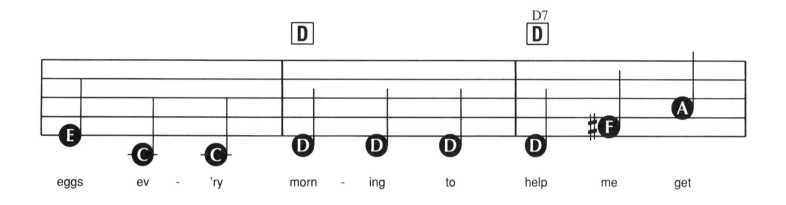

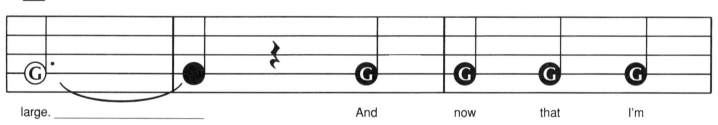

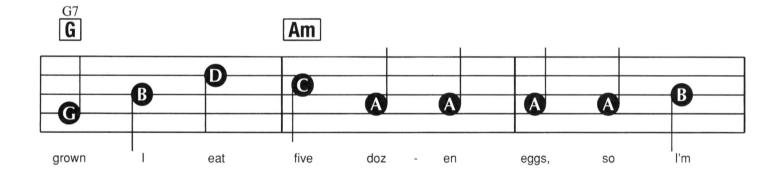

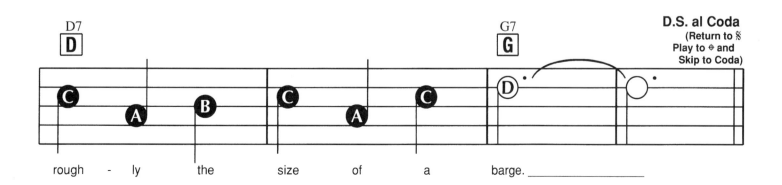

CODA

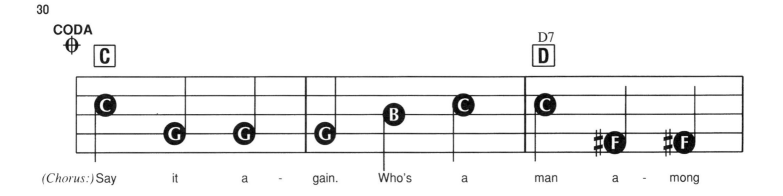

(Chorus:) Say it a - gain. Who's a man a - mong

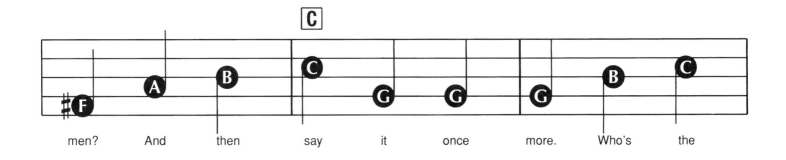

men? And then say it once more. Who's the

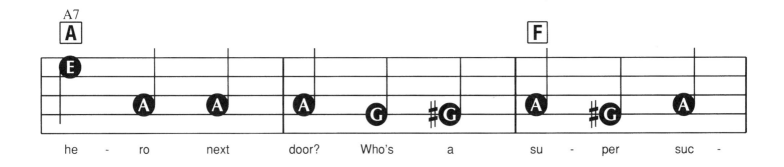

he - ro next door? Who's a su - per suc -

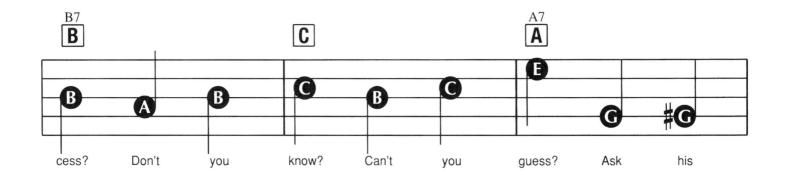

cess? Don't you know? Can't you guess? Ask his

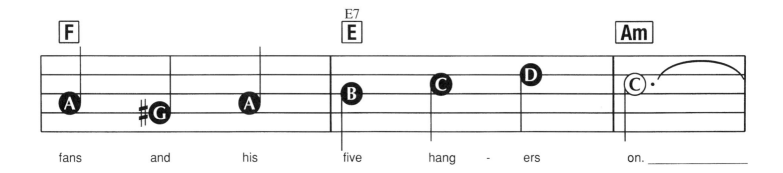

fans and his five hang - ers on. _____

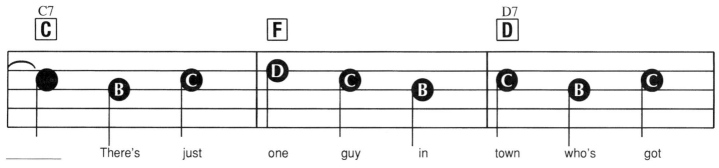

There's just one guy in town who's got

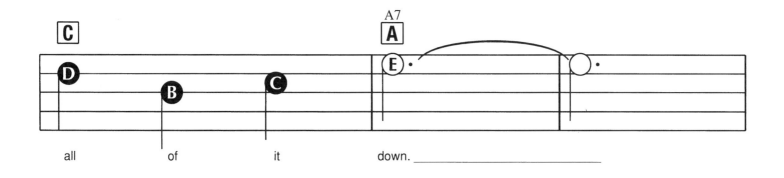

all of it down. _____

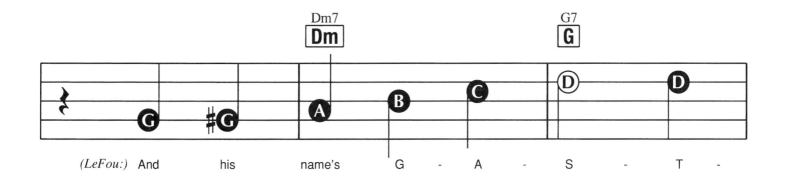

(LeFou:) And his name's G - A - S - T -

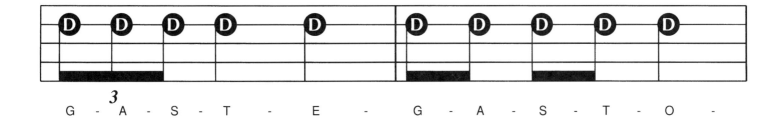

3
G - A - S - T - E - G - A - S - T - O -

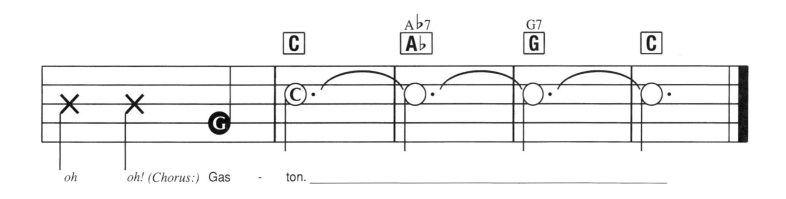

oh *oh!* *(Chorus:)* Gas - ton. _____

Be Our Guest

Registration 5
Rhythm: March or Polka

Music by Alan Menken
Lyrics by Howard Ashman

N.C.

Be our guest! Be our guest! Put our
gout! Cheese souf - flé! Pie and

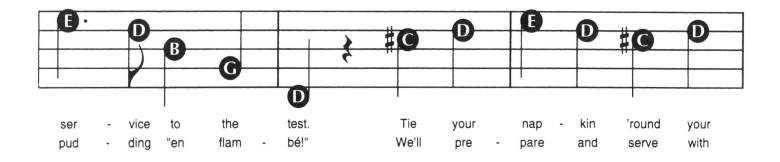

ser - vice to the test. Tie your nap - kin 'round your
pud - ding "en flam - bé!" We'll pre - pare and serve your with

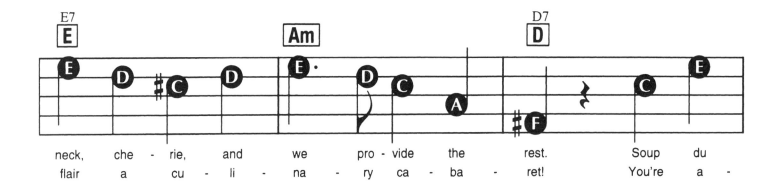

E7 Am D7

neck, che - rie, and we pro - vide the rest. Soup du
flair a cu - li - na - ry ca - ba - ret! You're a -

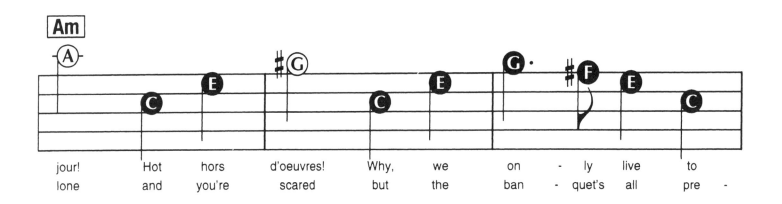

Am

jour! Hot hors d'oeuvres! Why, we on - ly live to
lone and you're scared but the ban - quet's all pre -

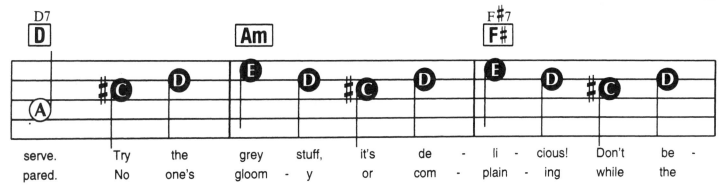

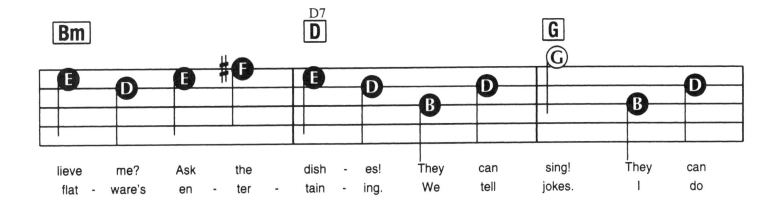

serve. Try the grey stuff, it's de - li - cious! Don't be -
pared. No one's gloom - y or com - plain - ing while the

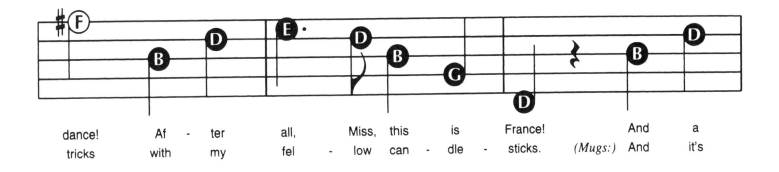

lieve me? Ask the dish - es! They can sing! They can
flat - ware's en - ter - tain - ing. We can tell jokes. I can

dance! Af - ter all, Miss, this is France! And a
tricks with my fel - low can - dle - sticks. *(Mugs:)* And it's

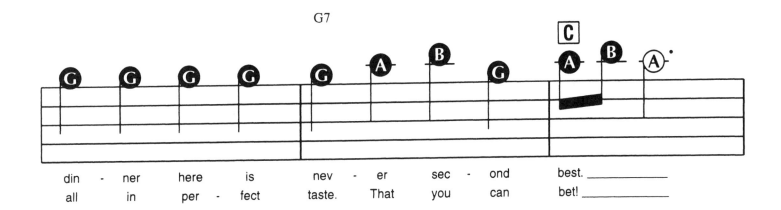

din - ner here is nev - er sec - ond best. _____
all in per - fect taste. That you can bet! _____

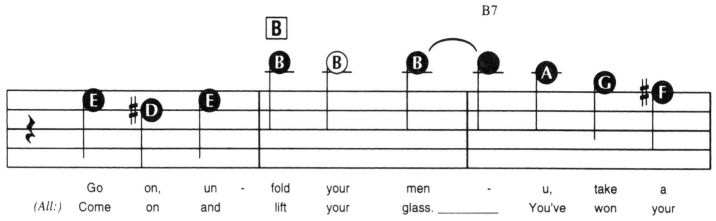

Go on, un - fold your men - u, take a
(All:) Come on and lift your glass. _____ You've won your

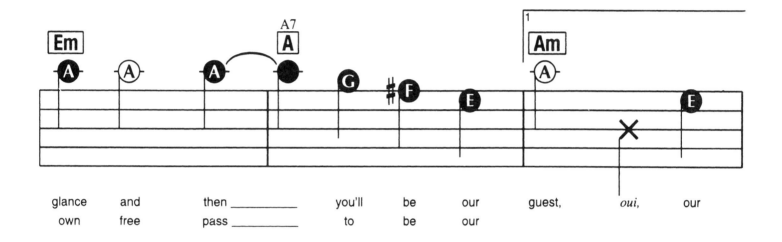

glance and then _____ you'll be our guest, *oui,* our
own and free pass _____ to be our

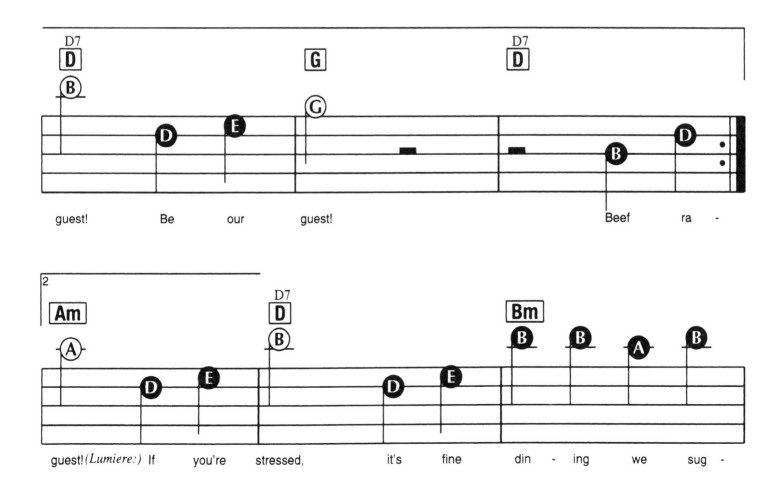

guest! Be our guest! Beef ra -

guest! *(Lumiere:)* If you're stressed, it's fine din - ing we sug -

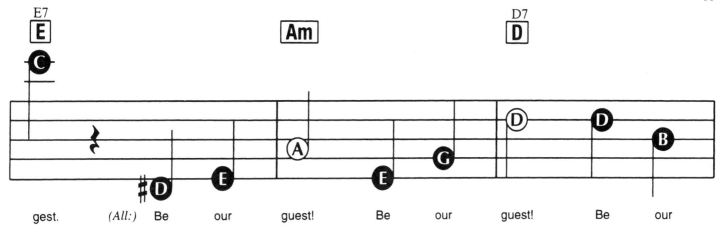

gest. *(All:)* Be our guest! Be our guest! Be our

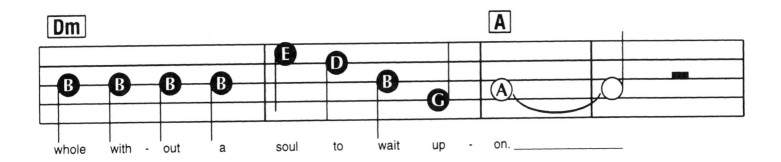

guest! *(Lumiere:)* Life is so un -

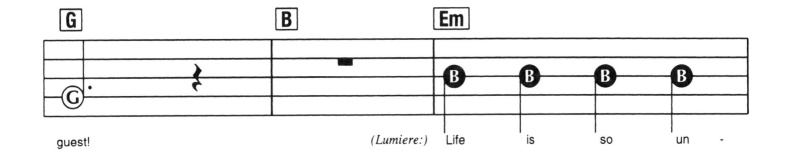

nerv - ing for a ser - vant who's not serv - ing. He's not

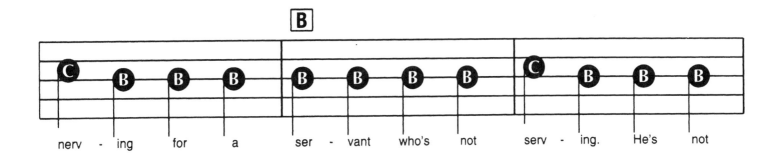

whole with - out a soul to wait up - on. _____

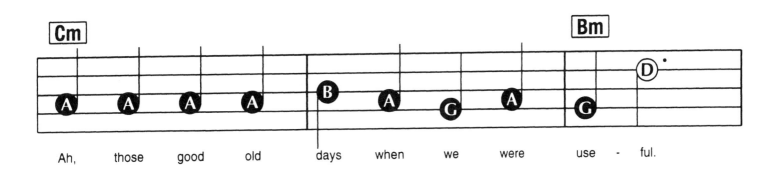

Ah, those good old days when we were use - ful.

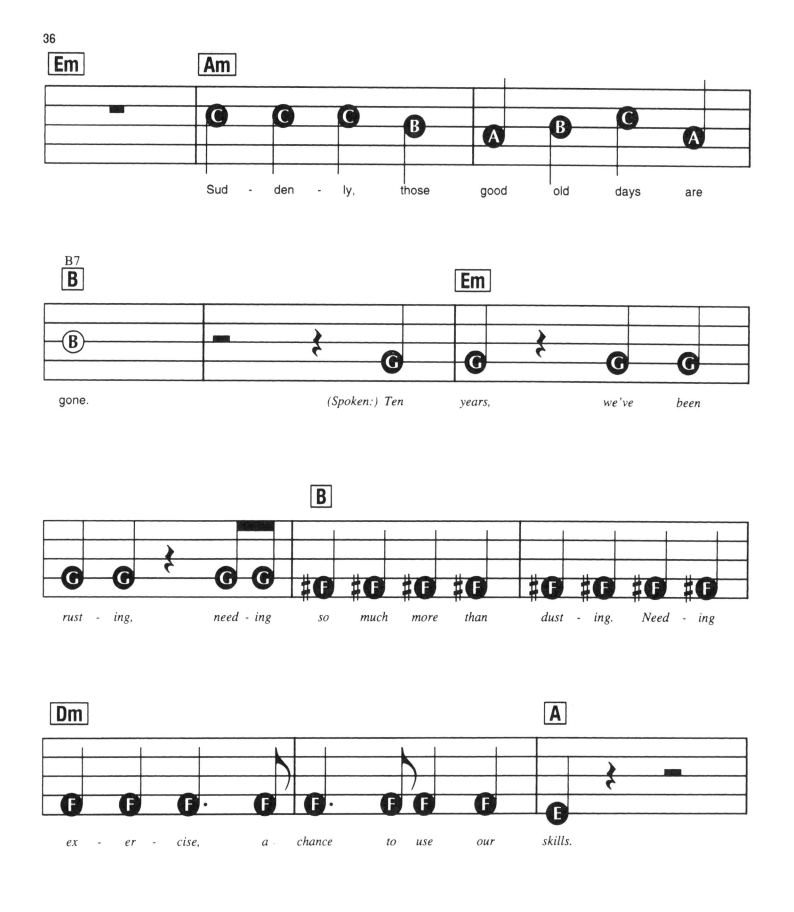

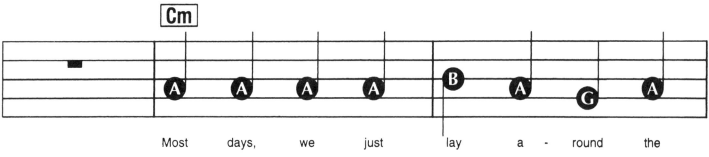

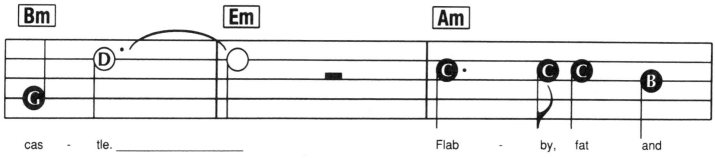

cas - tle. _____ Flab - by, fat and

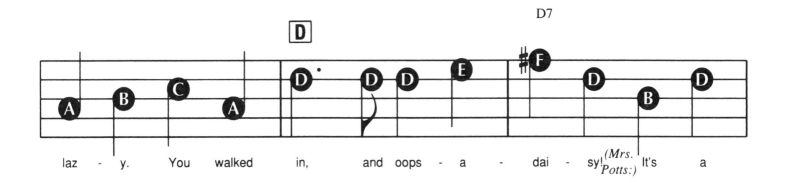

laz - y. You walked in, and oops - a - dai - sy! *(Mrs. Potts:)* It's a

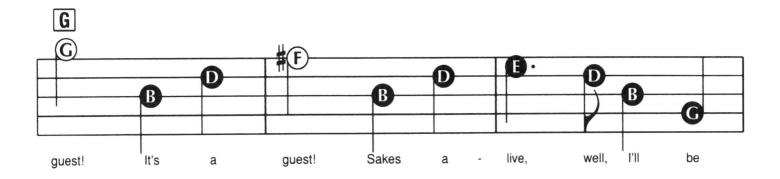

guest! It's a guest! Sakes a - live, well, I'll be

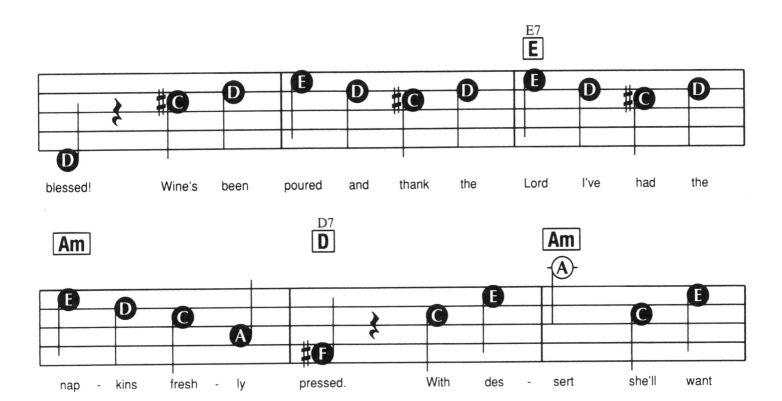

blessed! Wine's been poured and thank the Lord I've had the

nap - kins fresh - ly pressed. With des - sert she'll want

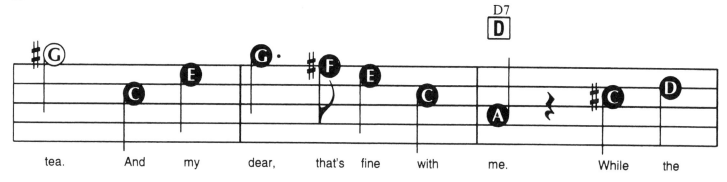

tea.   And   my   dear,   that's   fine   with   me.   While   the

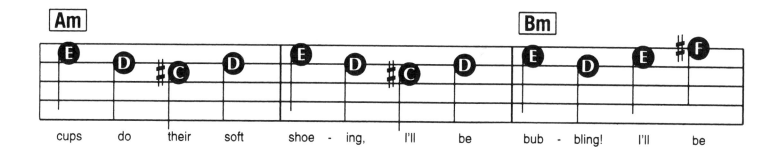

cups   do   their   soft   shoe - ing,   I'll   be   bub - bling!   I'll   be

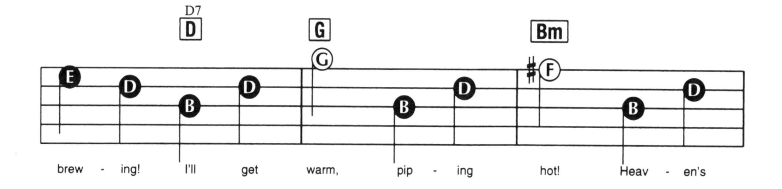

brew - ing!   I'll   get   warm,   pip - ing   hot!   Heav - en's

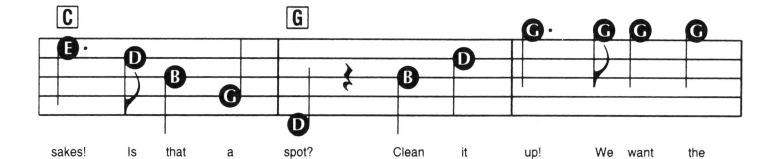

sakes!   Is   that   a   spot?   Clean   it   up!   We   want   the

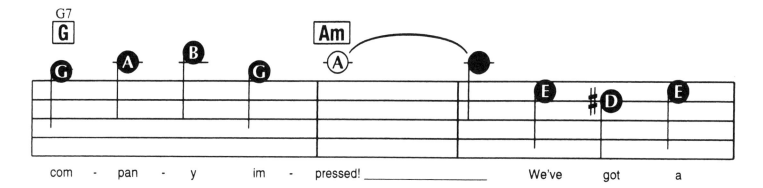

com - pan - y   im - pressed! _____   We've   got   a

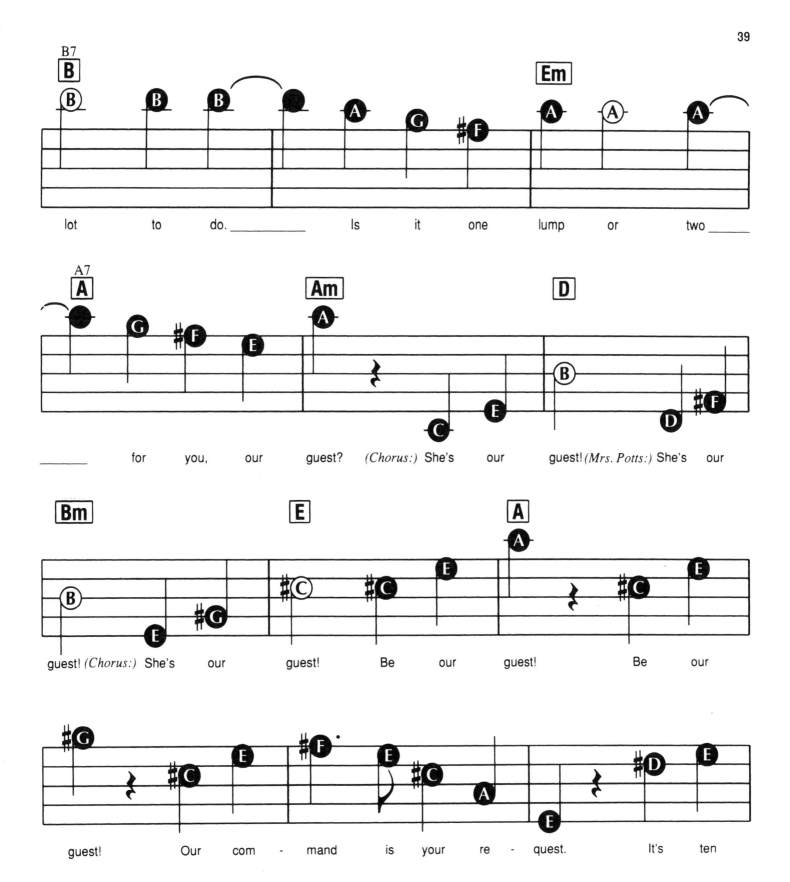

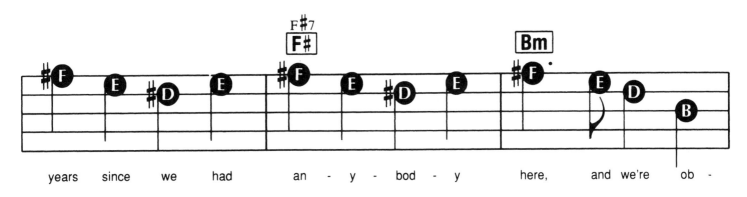

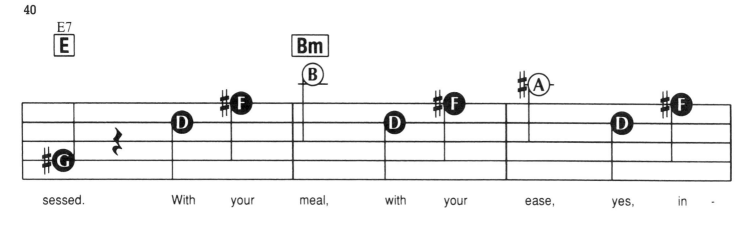

sessed.   With   your   meal,   with   your   ease,   yes,   in -

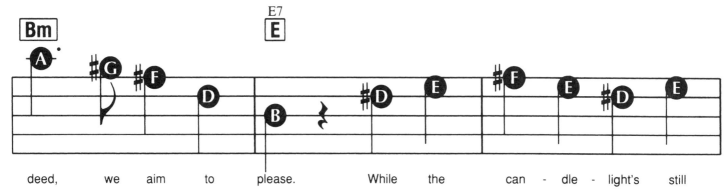

deed,   we   aim   to   please.   While   the   can - dle - light's   still

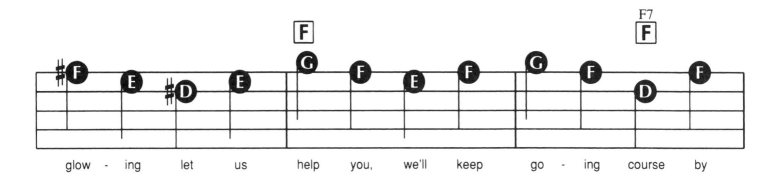

glow - ing   let   us   help   you,   we'll   keep   go - ing   course   by

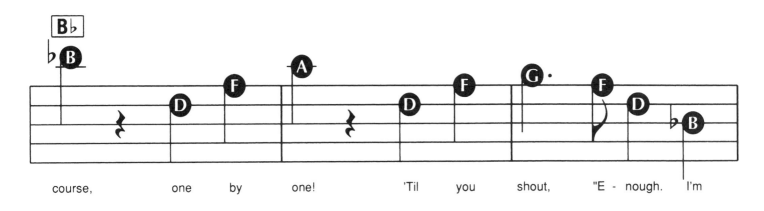

course,   one   by   one!   'Til   you   shout,   "E - nough.   I'm

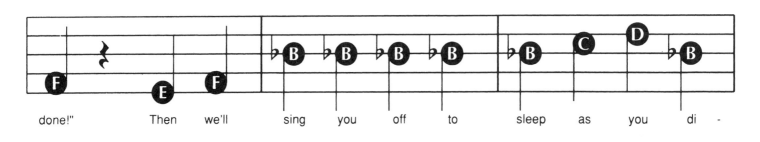

done!"   Then   we'll   sing   you   off   to   sleep   as   you   di -

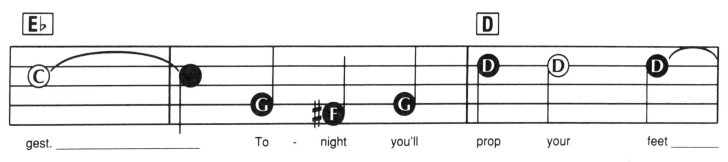

gest. _____ To - night you'll prop your feet _____

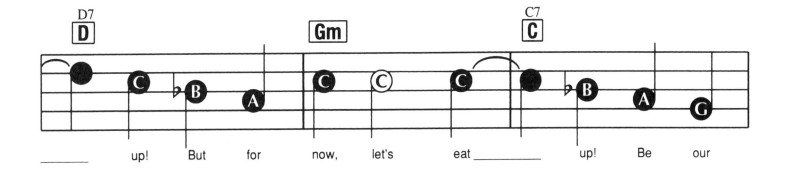

_____ up! But for now, let's eat _____ up! Be our

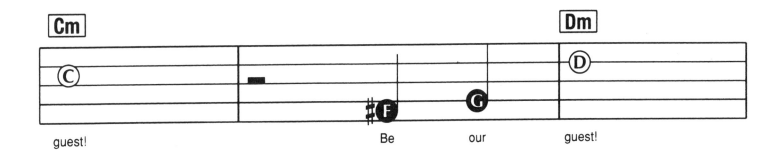

guest! Be our guest!

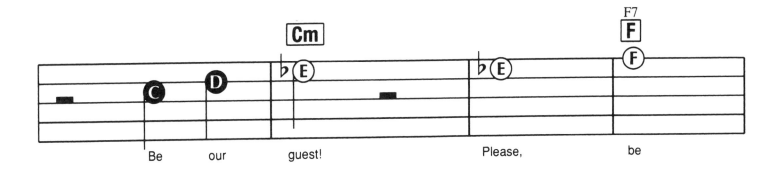

Be our guest! Please, be

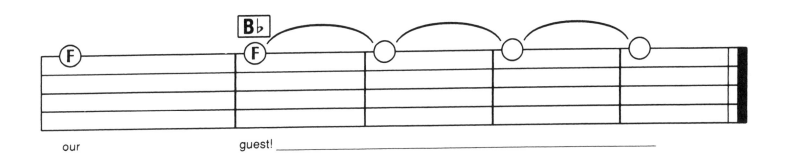

our guest! _____

Days in the Sun

Registration 3
Rhythm: Ballad

Music by Alan Menken
Lyrics by Tim Rice

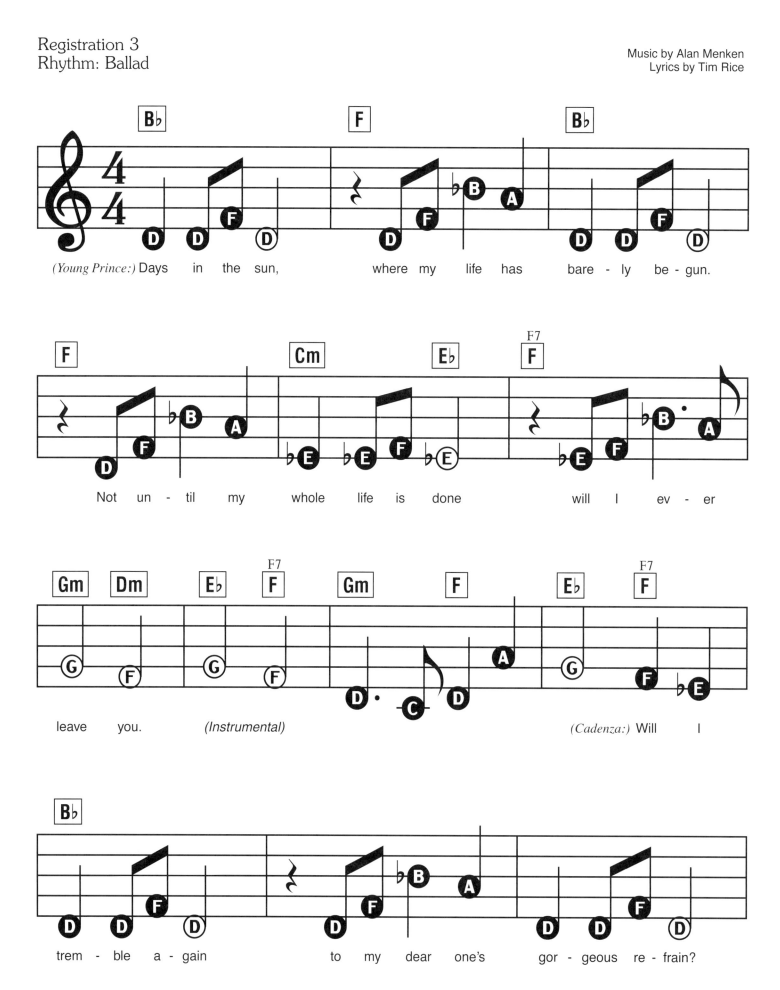

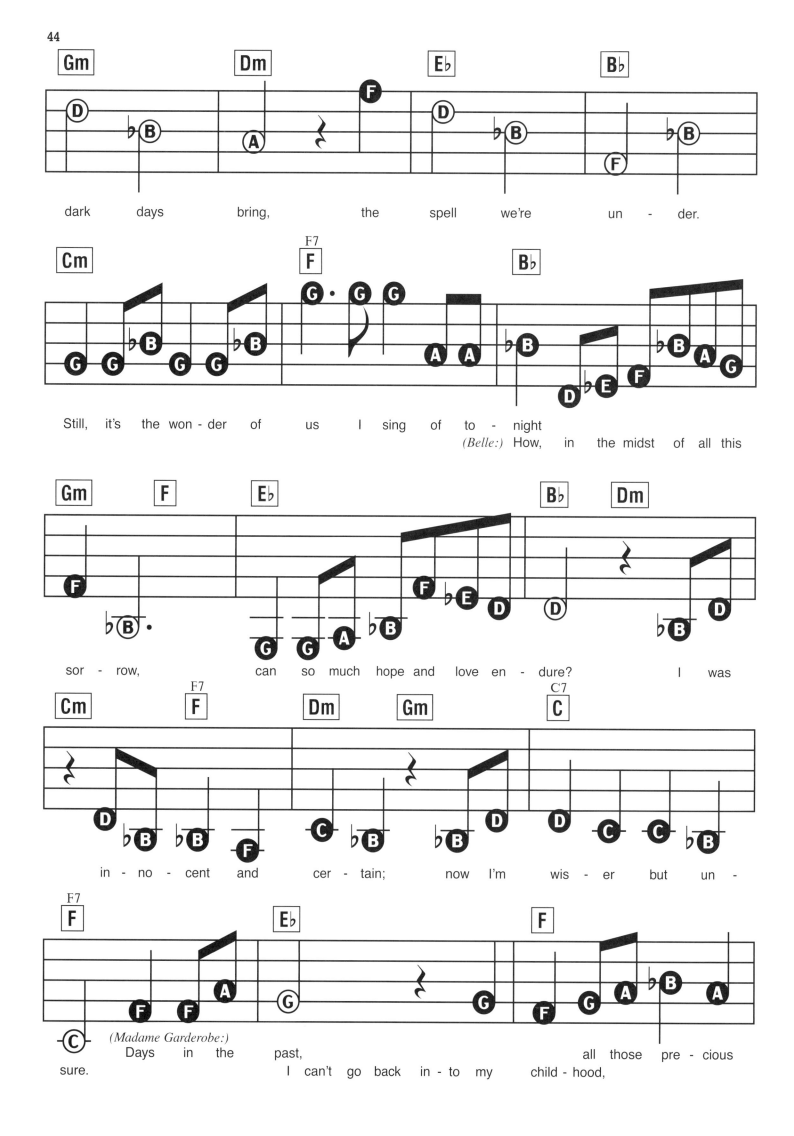

45

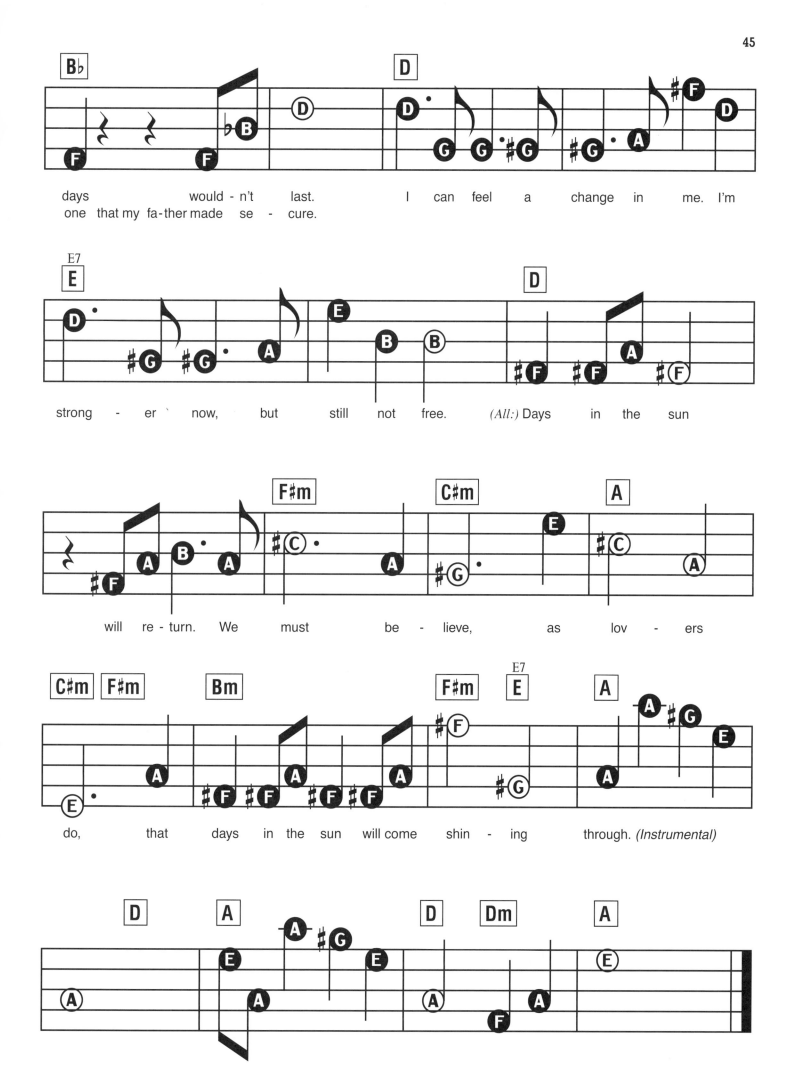

Something There

Registration 7
Rhythm: 8-Beat or Pops

Music by Alan Menken
Lyrics by Howard Ashman

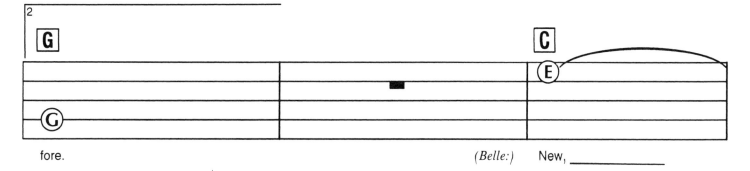

fore. *(Belle:)* New, _____

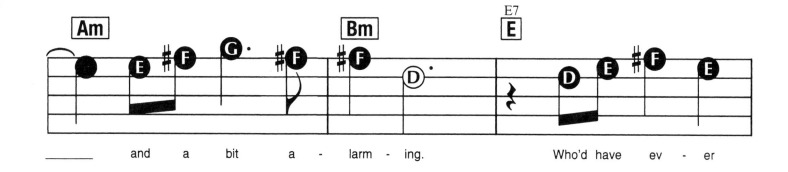

_____ and a bit a - larm - ing. Who'd have ev - er

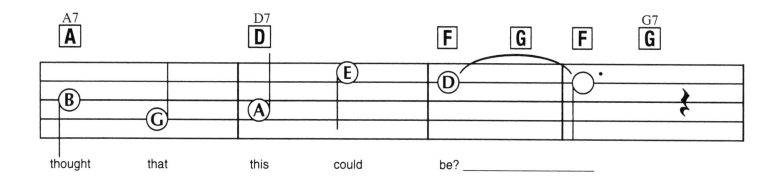

thought that this could be? _____

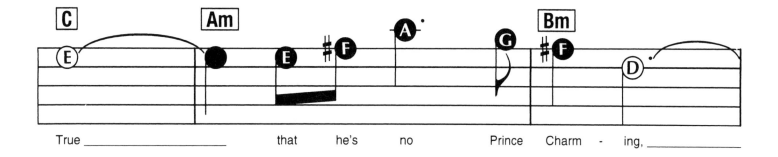

True _____ that he's no Prince Charm - ing, _____

48

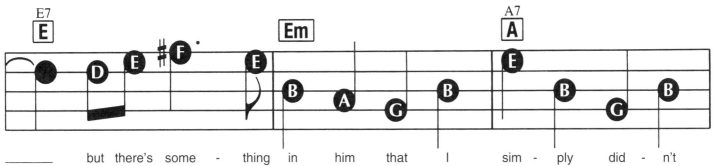

but there's some - thing in him that I sim - ply did - n't

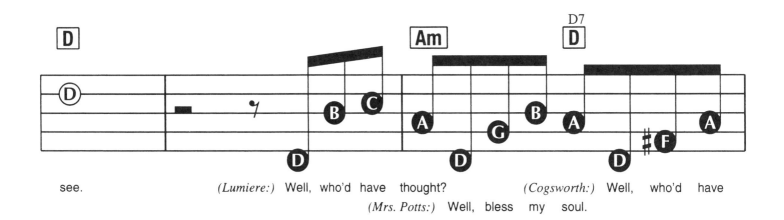

see.   (*Lumiere:*) Well, who'd have thought?   (*Cogsworth:*) Well, who'd have

(*Mrs. Potts:*) Well, bless my soul.

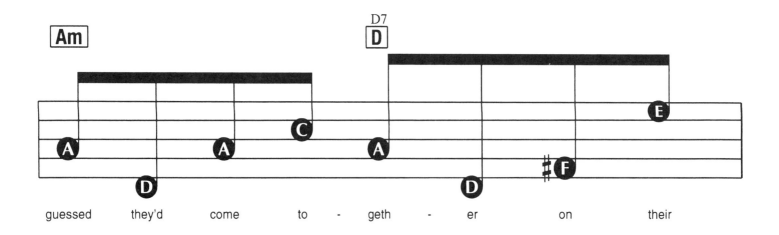

known?   (*Lumiere:*) And who'd have

Well, who in - deed?

guessed they'd come to - geth - er on their

49

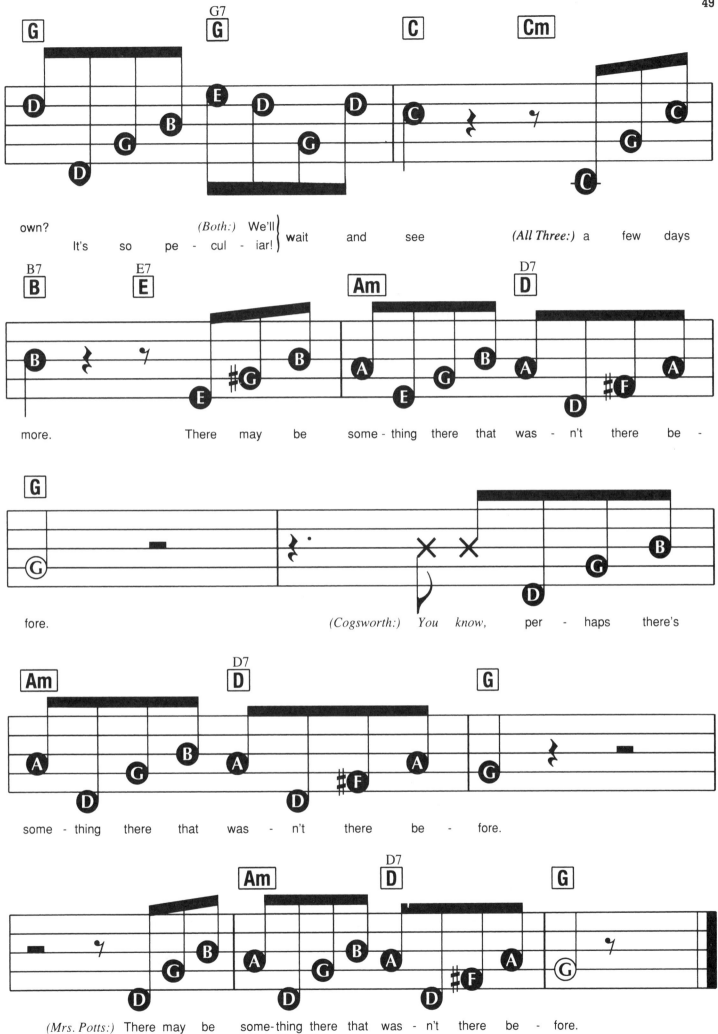

Beauty and the Beast

Registration 1
Rhythm: Pops or 8-Beat

Music by Alan Menken
Lyrics by Howard Ashman

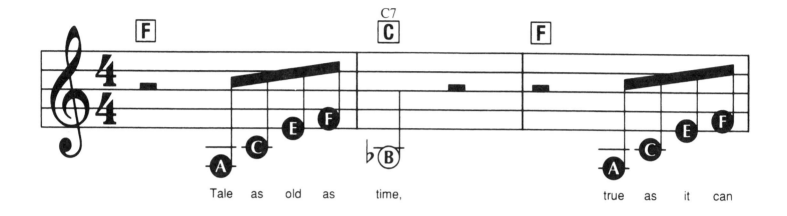

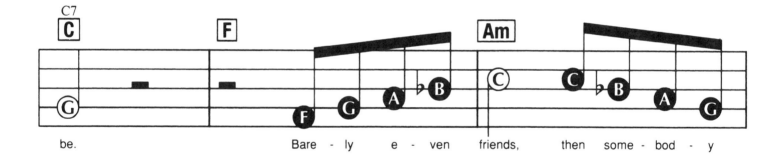

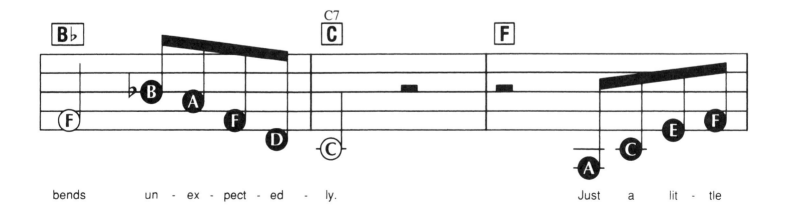

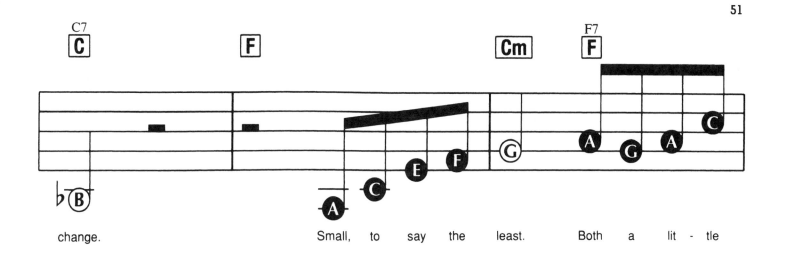

change.   Small, to say the least. Both a lit - tle

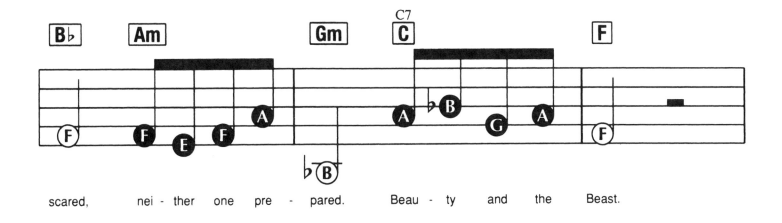

scared,   nei - ther one pre - pared.   Beau - ty   and   the   Beast.

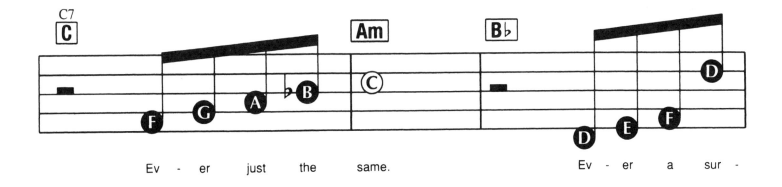

Ev - er   just   the   same.   Ev - er   a   sur -

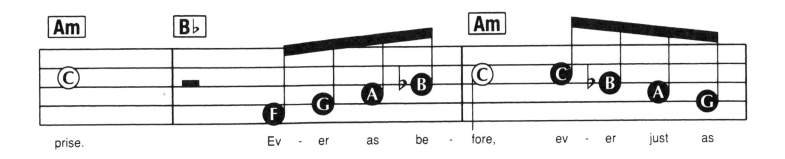

prise.   Ev - er   as   be - fore,   ev - er   just   as

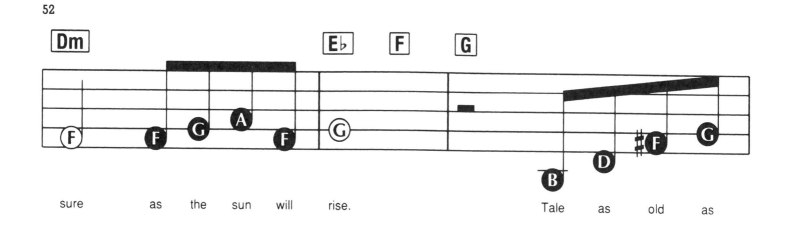

sure   as   the   sun will rise.   Tale   as old as

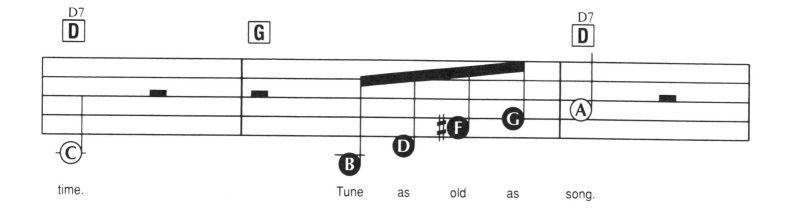

time.   Tune   as old as song.

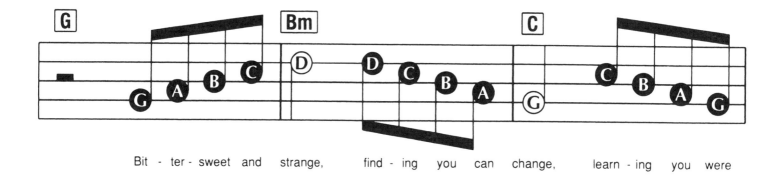

Bit - ter - sweet and strange,   find - ing you can change,   learn - ing you were

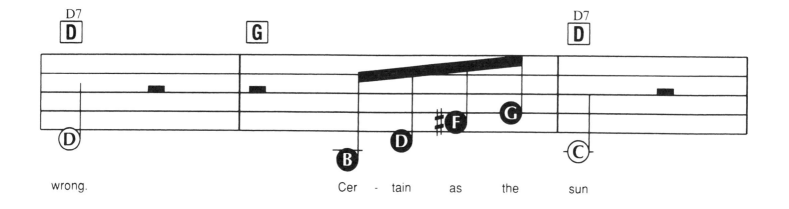

wrong.   Cer - tain as the sun

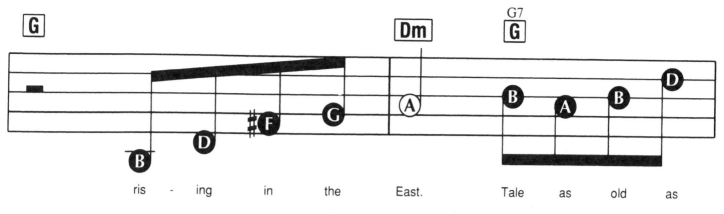

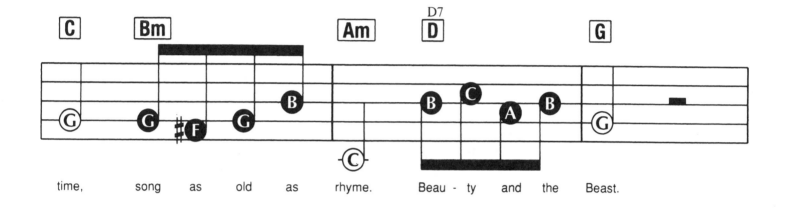

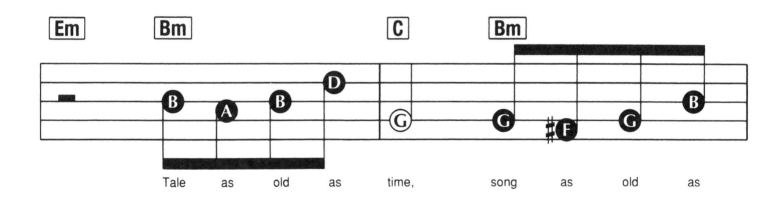

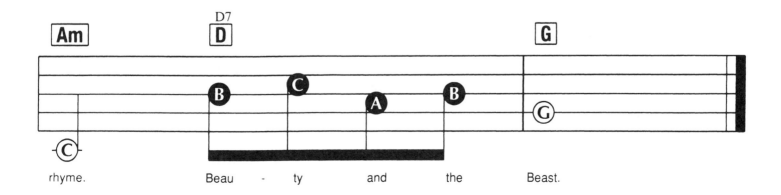

Evermore

Registration 2
Rhythm: Ballad

Music by Alan Menken
Lyrics by Howard Ashman

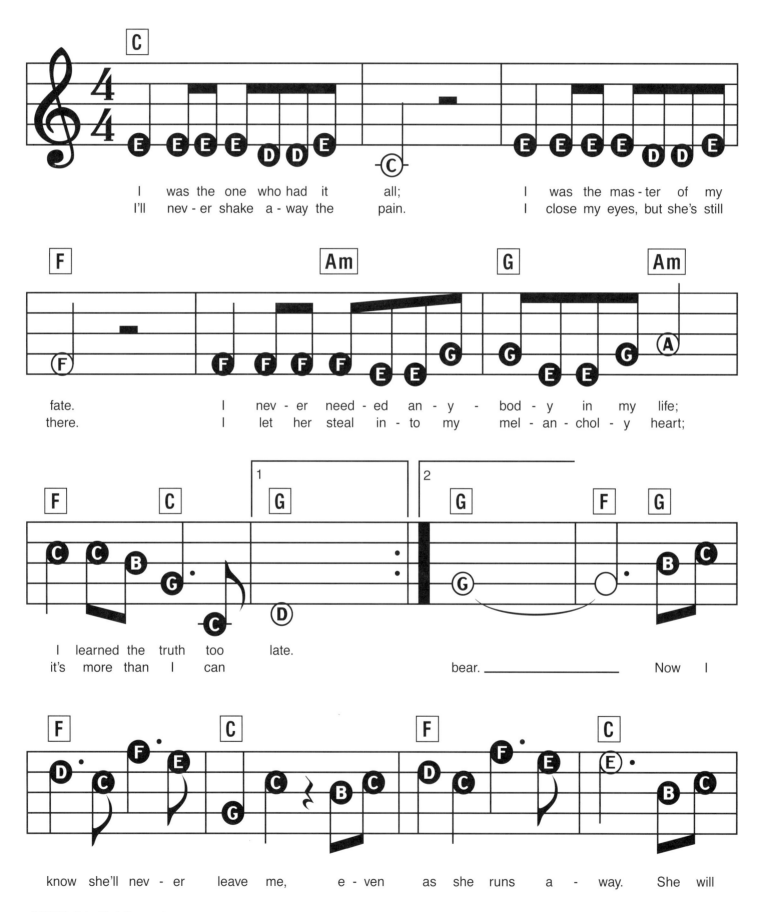

I was the one who had it all;
I'll nev-er shake a-way the pain.

I was the mas-ter of my
I close my eyes, but she's still

fate.
there.

I nev-er need-ed an-y-bod-y in my life;
I let her steal in-to my mel-an-chol-y heart;

I learned the truth too late.
it's more than I can

bear. _____ Now I

know she'll nev-er leave me, e-ven as she runs a-way. She will

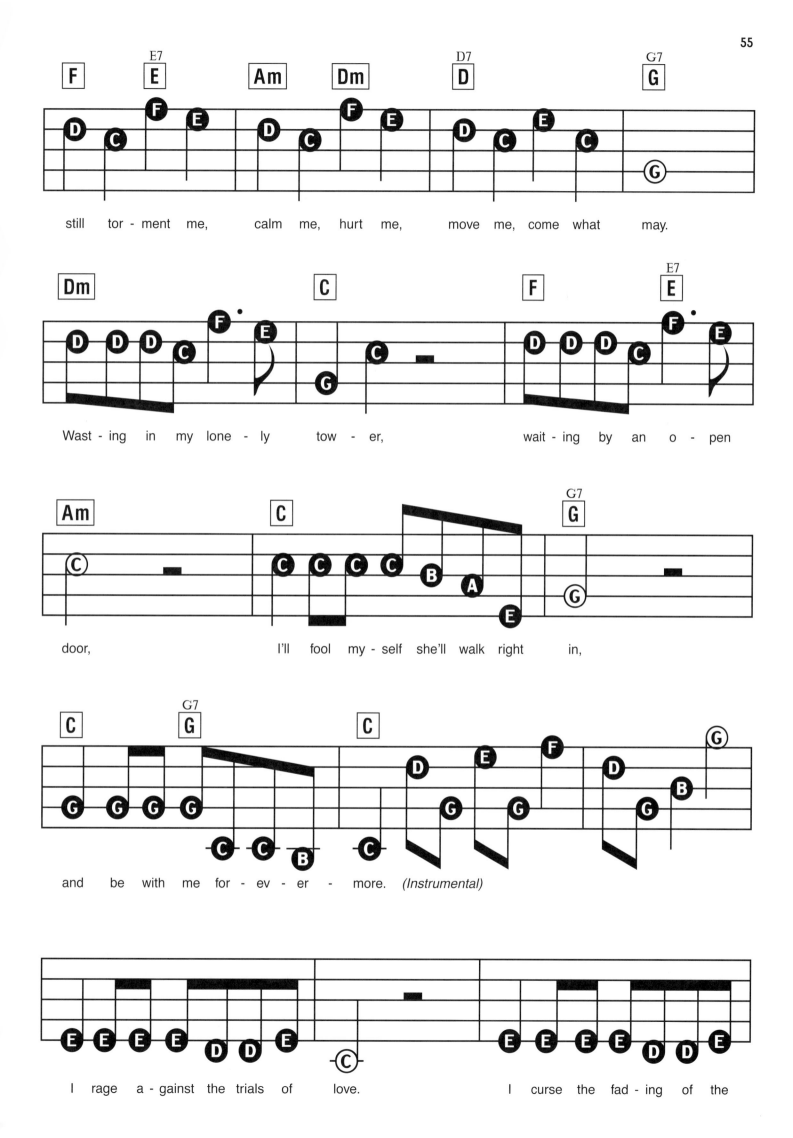

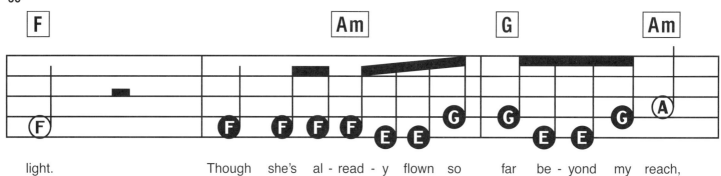

light. Though she's al - read - y flown so far be - yond my reach,

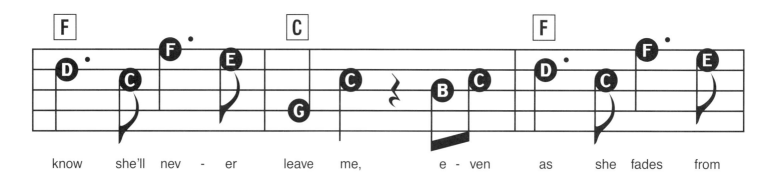

she's nev - er out of sight. Now I

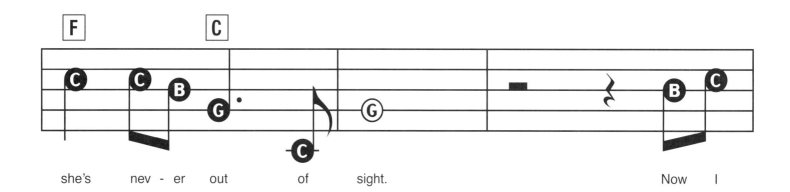

know she'll nev - er leave me, e - ven as she fades from

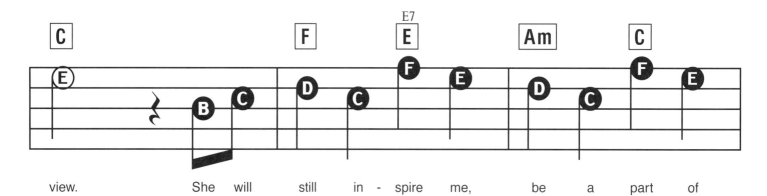

view. She will still in - spire me, be a part of

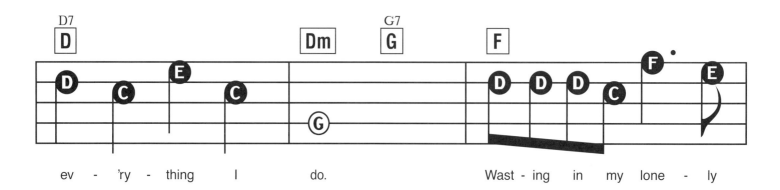

ev - 'ry - thing I do. Wast - ing in my lone - ly

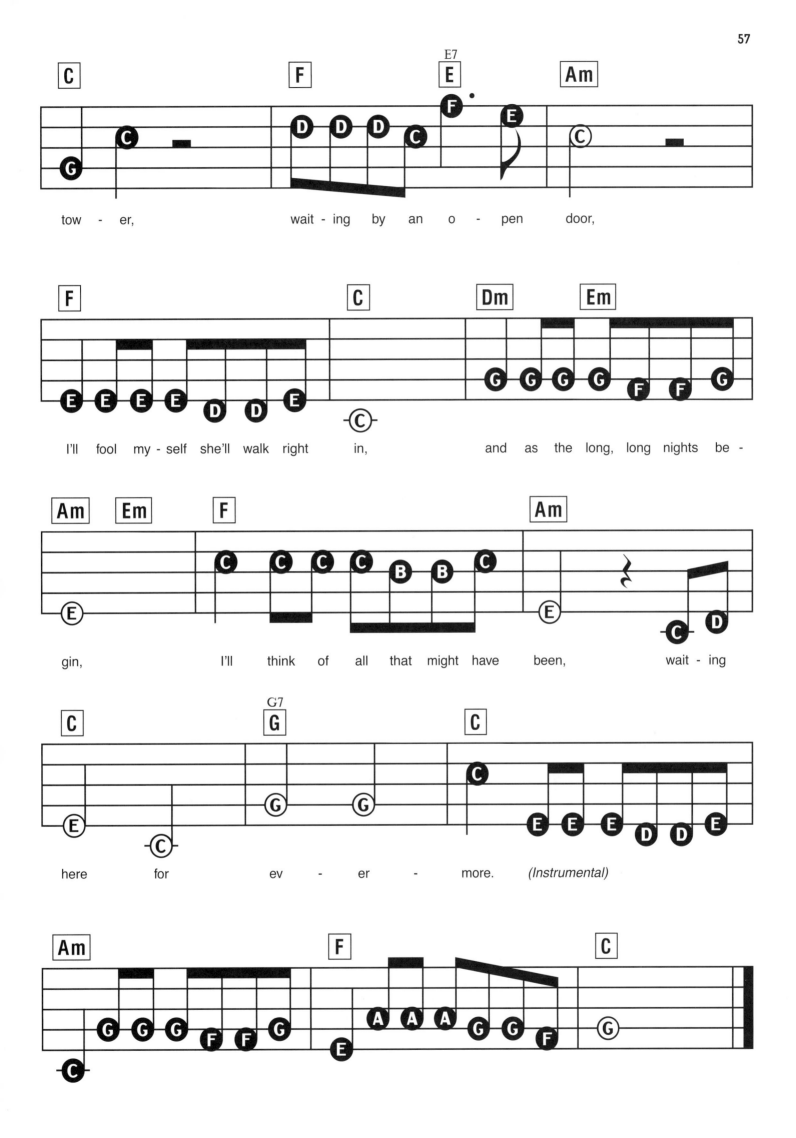

The Mob Song

Registration 9
Rhythm: March or Rock

Music by Alan Menken
Lyrics by Howard Ashman

(Man I:) We're not safe un - til he's dead. *(Man II:)* He'll come

stalk - ing us at night. *(Woman:)* Set to

sac - ri - fice our chil - dren to his

mon - strous ap - pe - tite. *(Man III:)* He'll wreak

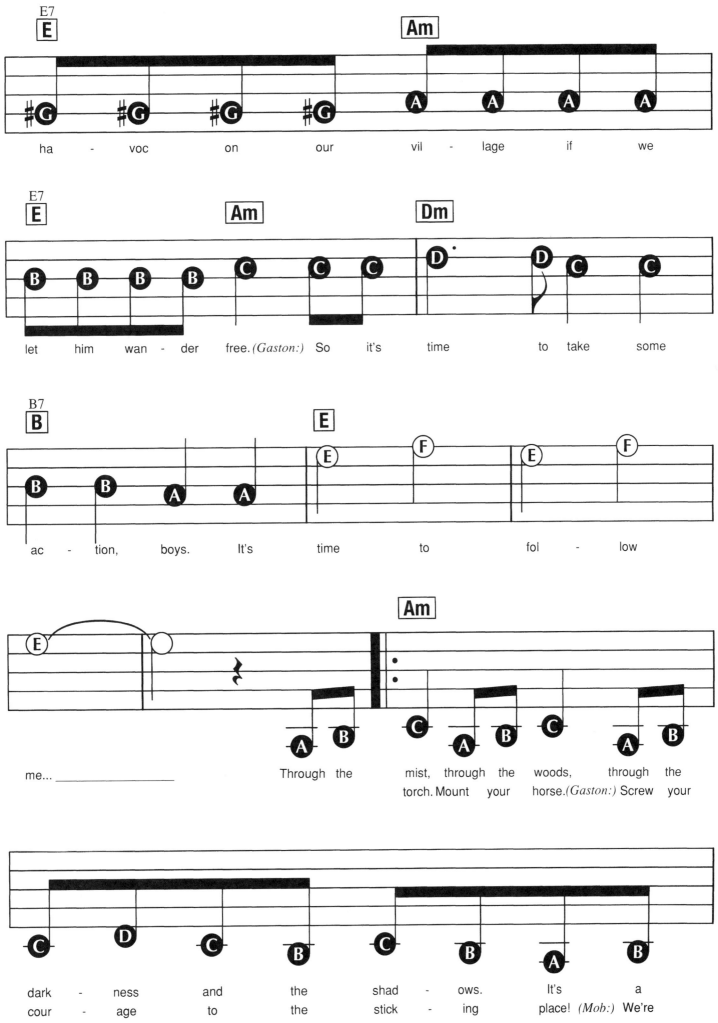

60

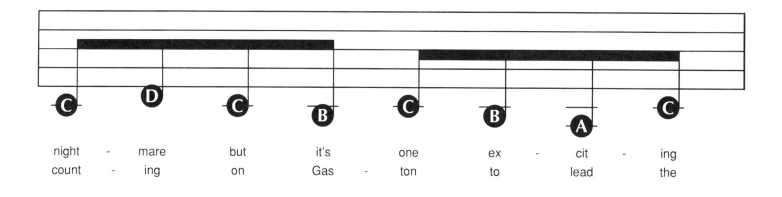

night - mare but it's one ex - cit - ing
count - ing on Gas - ton to lead the

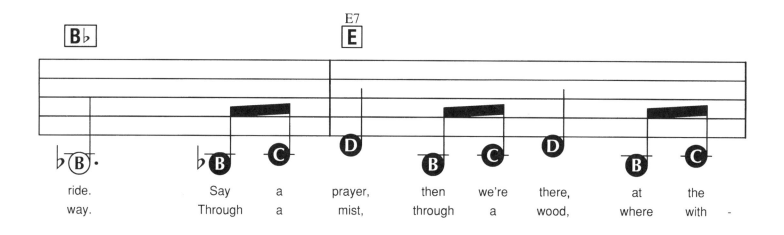

ride. Say a prayer, then we're there, at the
way. Through a mist, through a wood, where with -

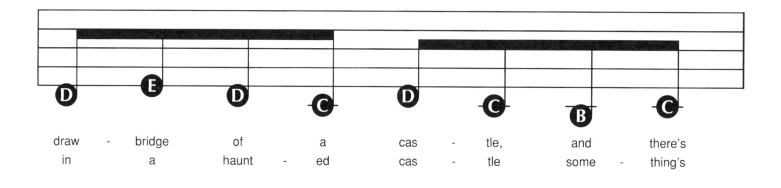

draw - bridge of a cas - tle, and there's
in a haunt - ed cas - tle some - thing's

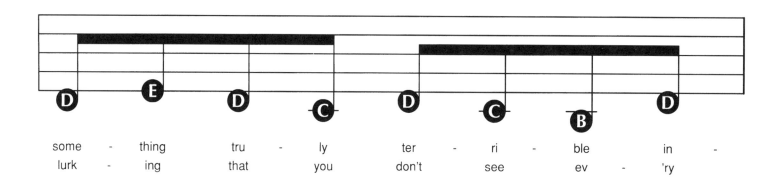

some - thing tru - ly ter - ri - ble in -
lurk - ing that you don't see ev - 'ry

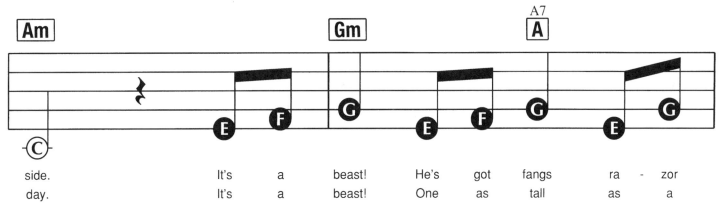

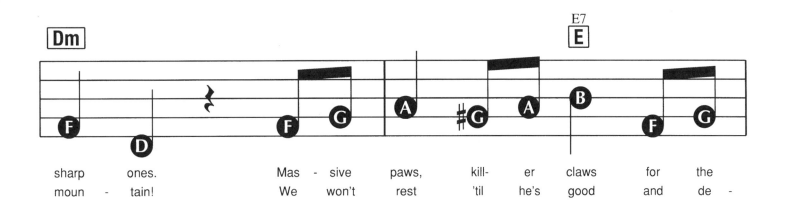

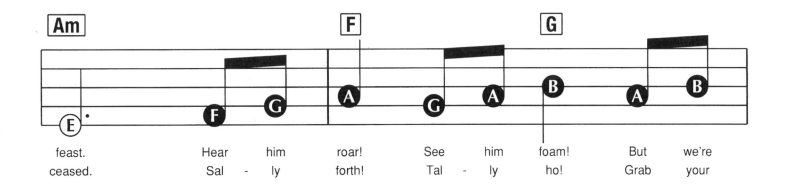

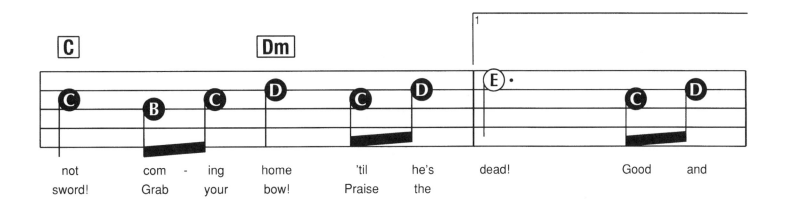

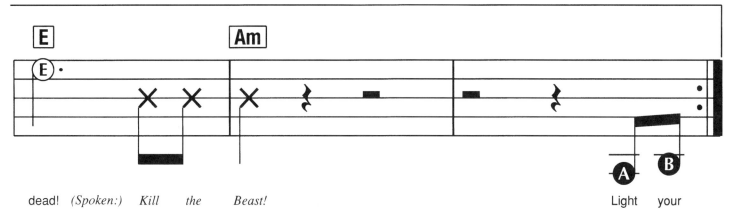

dead! *(Spoken:) Kill the Beast!* Light your

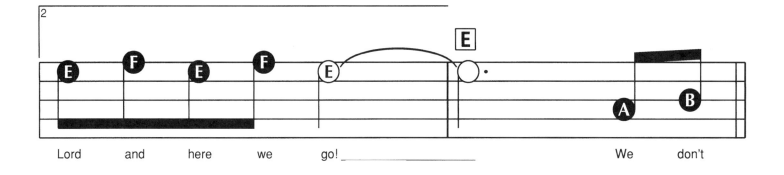

Lord and here we go! _____ We don't

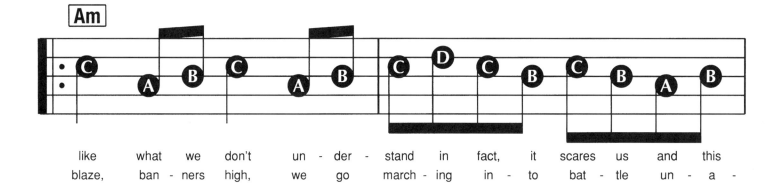

like what we don't un - der - stand in fact, it scares us and this
blaze, ban - ners high, we go march - ing in - to bat - tle un - a -

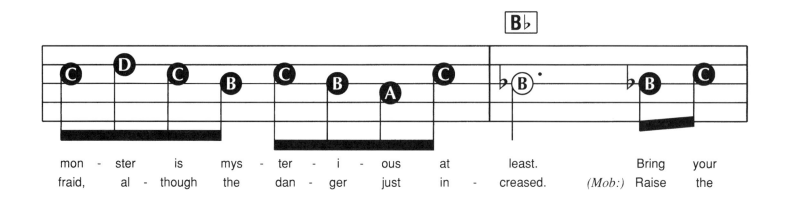

mon - ster is mys - ter - i - ous at least. Bring your
fraid, al - though the dan - ger just in - creased. *(Mob:)* Raise the

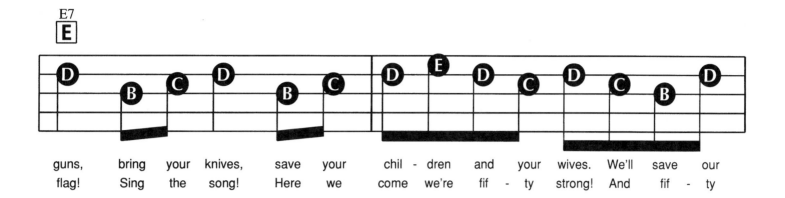

guns,   bring   your   knives,   save   your   chil - dren   and   your   wives.   We'll   save   our
flag!   Sing   the   song!   Here   we   come   we're   fif - ty   strong!   And   fif - ty

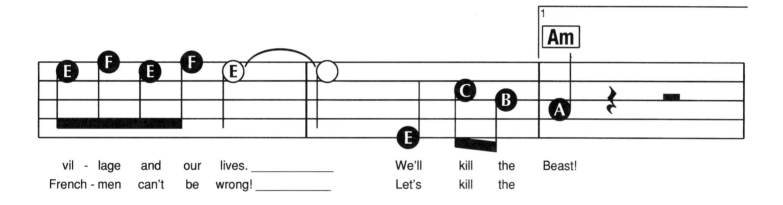

vil - lage   and   our   lives. _____   We'll   kill   the   Beast!
French - men   can't   be   wrong! _____   Let's   kill   the

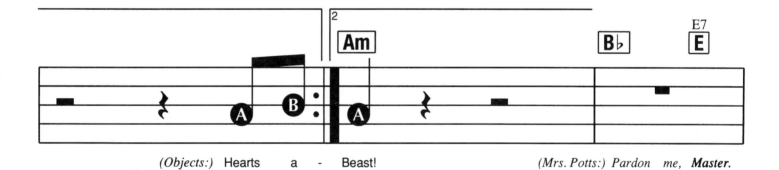

(Objects:) Hearts   a - Beast!   (Mrs. Potts:) Pardon   me,   **Master.**

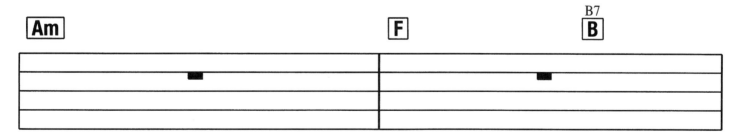

(Beast:) Leave   me   in   peace.   (Mrs. Potts:) But   sir,   the   castle

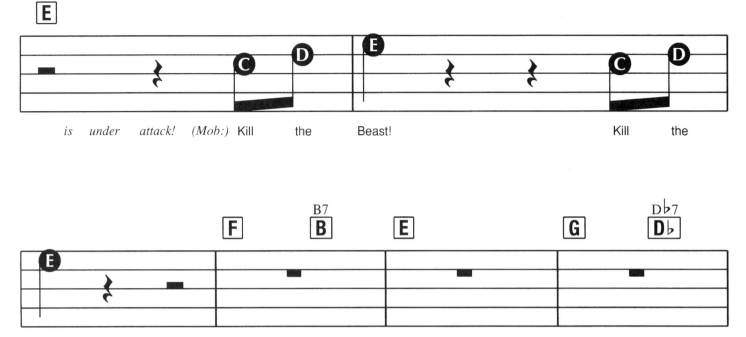

is under attack! *(Mob:)* Kill the Beast! Kill the

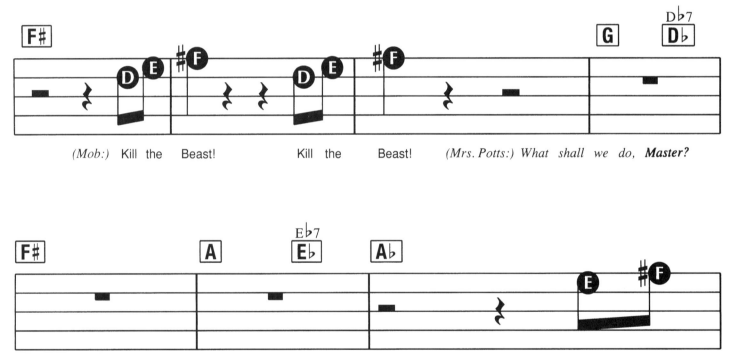

Beast!*(Lumiere:) This isn't working!(Featherduster:) Oh Lumiere. We must do something!(Lumiere:) Wait, I know!*

(Mob:) Kill the Beast! Kill the Beast! *(Mrs. Potts:)* What shall we do, **Master?**

(Beast:) It doesn't matter now. Just let them come. *(Mob:)* Kill the

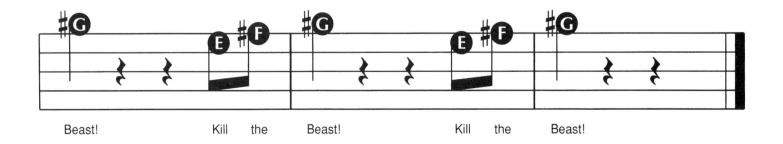

Beast! Kill the Beast! Kill the Beast!